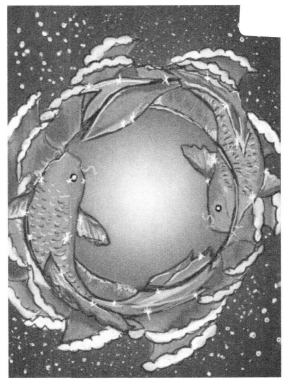

Pisces, you are the empath my dear Old Soul...
you're wise, modest, caring and whole.
You are one of the few signs truly balanced,
spiritual, down-to-earth, & humble; yet advanced.

You are magnetic, sensitive and so very deep,
a dreamer and mystic with a real love of sensuality.
You are *extra*ordinary, gifted creatively with evolved imagination,
but you don't abuse your powers of insight or persuasion.

See, you truly are the most spiritual sign around,
you know when to vibrate high and when to stay close to earth & ground.
Psychic, empathic, kind and generous; holistically complete,
you're a real gem & diamond to every soul you meet.

Divinity flows through you- you're tuned into cosmic energies,
and you can access subtle dimensions for ancient wisdom & memory.
Kindness, caring, unconditional love and powerful instincts flows through your
veins; an empath and multi-talented, you came here to change the game.

# Contents

## Acknowledgements

I dedicate this book to all the people, animals, nature & celestial entities who shaped my journey.

A true Pisces is at one with the earth and universe... Life is magical, and for this I offer my gratitude to the miracle that is life.

In Oneness and grace.

## Background to the Author

I wrote this just before my 29th birthday, as a Pisces, with Venus in Pisces too, who came from a very closed off and emotional background. My childhood and youth was rich in creativity, imaginative & artistic outlets, and educational doorways. My Leo mother provided me with many physical and material pathways for success and growth, but, quite simply, I was a very sensitive child. I felt misunderstood and like the 'oddball' - or 'black sheep' of the family. If you know anything about astrology, you will know that being a super-sensitive Pisces child with a Leo mother is not wholly compatible or harmonious. Leo is masculine while Pisces is feminine. Leo can also be too overpowering and dominant for the Piscean nature, it's just fundamental differences in character. My dad is (or was?) a Pisces too, although I barely knew him. He chose not to be in my life... I intuitively feel some key themes in *rejection* around this, ancestral and karmic wounds associated with Pisces' greatest fear... rejection.

I dreamt a lot and daydreamed often. I was sensitive, very emotional, artistic and dreamy. I remember having vivid dreams in my childhood and early teenage years. They would be quite dark, yet I was seldom scared; I quite enjoyed the darkness. Later in life I came to realize the darkness is symbolic of the astral & subconscious realms, shamanic forces too. So I guess I instinctively recognized the darkness of the dream worlds as a gateway to my soul. There was nothing to fear. As a Pisces, I always felt at home in the dreamworlds long before I ever read a book on what was occurring. Of course, not all dreams were dark. I had some truly magical and light-infused dreams, with celestial light beings, angels, mermaids and magic.... More on this later.

So, I was always a sensitive soul growing up. Looking back, now at age 29 with years of growth and self-development, wisdom and higher perspective, I can honestly say I dealt with a lot that no one would ever know. Some people can't comprehend it either. The thing about Pisces is: we have a *very* rich inner world. On the outside we may appear uninterested, shy, dull or simply quiet; yet inside there are swirling galaxies and portals to cosmic consciousness. Pisces sign is deeply in tune with the subconscious realms where imagery, insight, and symbolism are rich and strong.

Thus, I suffered a lot in silence. I would give myself tests, trials and personal milestones for growth and transformation. I created worlds inside my dreams that I would return to over and over, until I mastered the lesson and didn't need to visit anymore. Self-mastery was integral to my childhood. I'm not sure whether I did this on some conscious level, or if it was my soul doing it naturally (organically), but it happened all the same. As a Pisces, I recognize that life is a game. Consciousness is the primary force of life, waking life is only one aspect of "reality." Something a non-water sign may not realize... We feel things *deeply*. Water signs actually exist on a different level to the other signs. We're attuned to a different frequency, an emotional, empathic and psychic one. Gifts such as telepathy, psychic ability, clairvoyance and fine-tuned intuition come naturally to us. We are genuinely concerned with the suffering of others, the planet, animals and humanity as a whole- our compassion and empathy is developed to the max. I remember one dream I had so vividly, close to twenty or more times, of a classroom in a 'cosmic holographic chamber.' Some people from my youth were there, (now) old friends. There were lots of desks and a test. This test was a cosmic test of spiritual enlightenment and universal lessons. It was about life cycles and lessons, key insights into spiritual awakening, and consciousness- the "big realizations" relating to life's mysteries & meanings!

For a long period over the span of a few years the focus would be on me, I would sit down and take the test, always feeling a bit "spacey" and still very much in my shadowy self (typical young Pisces trait). It was a hard test. I would then be in a different dream scene where there was an otherworldly feel, again, very common for a Pisces. The first few times were really spacey and clearly unsuccessful. I never completed it. Then, I would pass quicker and quicker until I eventually completed the test multiple times. *The message*: the lessons were being integrated, I was learning and evolving. Each time I returned the test got easier, I was in the classroom for a shorter period of time, until I no longer had the dream… This was at a period of my life where my creativity and new connections aligned to my new path, my true service and soul purpose were soaring. This same dream occurred over the period of a couple of years; the very last time I had that dream I knew I had reached a completely "New Level," in my personal professional, emotional, spiritual and physical life. A less evolved and not so spiritually mature younger friend was there. She was taking the test for the first time. While I had already sat the same test over and over, for years having always completed it and passing with top marks, 100% (representing my spiritual wisdom and awareness, *Pisces is the most spiritual sign*, after all), she was in the beginning phase of her spiritual cycle. It was new to her, and she was stuck. I was there to guide her and be her divine assistance, an angelic helper in the dream worlds.

In my childhood I remember feeling so strange and peculiar in class. I was intelligent, that's one thing many people overlook. They think we're unintelligent because of how sensitive or dreamy we can be. Yet I was always at the top of my classes. I would think things contrary to the "norm" and develop my own beliefs & philosophies that were rooted in unconditional love. Topics and debates were always a chance for self-reflection, and regardless of whether I shared my viewpoints or not I knew strongly that I was destined to change and help the world in some way. Pisces are *visionaries. Changemakers*. We believe in the power of unity consciousness and unconditional love.

It wasn't until my early, mid and late twenties that I truly began to see the evolution of the Pisces spirit. My own journey is reflected in the collective journey. This may be my personal beliefs or it could be 'ultimate truth,' either way, it's my understanding of the human experience. Individual consciousness and collective are one and the same; the individual journey is reflected in the cosmic, universal story and vice versa. Looking back, I was a repressed, depressed and sad young girl with a lot on my shoulders. I suffered far more than I needed to, and things I read back in my youth that were once reacted to with, "yeah right!" actually were true. Pisces takes on the world's suffering. We're so empathic that we lose all sense of boundaries and merge with the pain, sorrow, and trauma of others. It can be quite depressing. Whilst other children and teenagers are out playing and socializing, partying or living carefree with a bounce in their step, many Pisces choose to go down the self-sacrificial route. There is a "heaviness" to this emotional sign. The other side of this highly introspective, suppressed and self-sacrificial world is the wisdom and strengths developed, of course. Through choosing to embody such a high emotional frequency (linked to compassion, healing, unconditional love, etc.), and focusing on self-mastery, wisdom acquisition, study, talent mastery, creative & artistic gifts, and spiritual awakening; we create a new energetic blueprint within and around. *We become the change we wish to see.*

Yes, my childhood was suppressed and full of emotional sensitivities. I was shy, reserved, and cut off from society and friendship circles more than I would have previously admitted. I was also prone to the addictions and escapist tendencies shared later. But, I was also a creative genius, highly empathic and perceptive, and on a real lifelong journey of self-evolution, of spiritual gifts and soul talents. My dreams, of course, simultaneously soared…

"We do not assume that each new-born animal creates its own instincts...
and we must not suppose that human individuals invent their specific
human ways with every new birth. Like the instincts, the collective
thought patterns of the human mind are innate and inherited."

~Carl Jung

# INTRODUCTION

*If you want to go straight to Pisces, cut the intro out.*

Dreaming is a fascinating thing. Dreams provide a portal into your subconscious mind. They shine a light on hidden desires, emotions, beliefs, feelings and memories that have made a strong impression in your life. Dreams will be different for everyone- every star sign has different dream themes and symbols that show up regularly for them. The way a *Pisces* dreams, for example, is completely unique. Rare, even. The subconscious provides deep insights into your true self. They are the root of spiritual growth, overcoming health issues, emotional balance and self-awareness. You can take a deep look into the hidden and unseen things, the "invisible" realms that lie just below the surface of your conscious mind. You can choose to consciously seek out messages, signs, symbols and hidden meanings too, and this is what leads to wonderful transformation. Health and well-being can equally be determined, as can revelations into your past, present and future.

So, what is a dream? A dream is a series of thoughts, images, emotions, moods and environments. Dreams can show us parts of our deepest selves, of our psyches, hidden wants and desires, fears and weaknesses, and of our internal impressions, emotions and currents. Dreams are ultimately gateways into the soul and into our whole self. They are here to show us what "vibratory state" we're operating at, and if we're going in the right direction. *'Am I aligned to my true path?' 'What is emotional frequency right now?' 'Is my health on point?' 'Am I still holding onto past wounds?' 'What needs to heal and be released in my life?'* These are just a few questions the subconscious mind brings to light. Furthermore, dreams can help you access your *soul gifts and talents*. As is the case with Pisces, the 12th and final sign of the Zodiac, dreaming can lead to much more than this as well. One can travel to unseen worlds, unique places of the soul and psyche, and engage in precognitive or prophetic dreaming for healing, sight and divine inspiration or assistance. All in all, dreams are a pathway of self-discovery, inspiration, and personal (and collective) awakening.

### *A brief history of dreaming*

People have been dreaming for thousands of years. 5000 years ago in Mesopotamia the earliest recorded writings of dreams were found. You may have heard of the "25,000 clay tablets..." Well, these came from the oldest living library and dreams were significantly mentioned. Ancient Egyptians were also very connected to their dreams; they had dream temples just like the Ancient Greeks. Dream temples served as places people could go for healing and to connect to their subconscious selves, through the power of *conscious dreaming*. Ancient Indian and Tibetan texts depicted the importance and power of dreams too, specifically as a tool for spiritual enlightenment. The Christian Bible shares God appearing before men and prophets, i.e. spiritually and psychically/astrally aware people, in dreams. Tibetan Buddhists believe dreams are portals or gateways for realizing illusion after death. There is a reason why Hippocrates was and still is known as the father of Greek medicine- one of his famous writings was called "On Dreams," and ancient Greece was one of the first few cultures in more modern times (i.e. not going as far back as Sumeria and Mesopotamia) that suggested prophetic, diagnostic and psychologically and spiritually revealing dreams were real. The father of modern philosophy Plato was also a big believer in dreams.

So, it's clear dreams and dreaming are a huge part of our human timeline. As we explore next in the Power of the Subconscious Mind, you will see why!

### *Interesting facts about dreaming?*

- People who have been blind from birth have dreams formed from other senses, including touch, smell and sound.
- Dolphins have the ability to switch off half of their brains…
- Elephants sleep standing up during non-REM sleep (but lie down for REM sleep). As can many other animals.
- During a lifetime, the average person spends about *six years* dreaming. This is, of course, much more in Pisces, the *Dreamer* of the Zodiac.

## The Power of the Subconscious Mind

Dreams are the gateway to your true self, to a higher consciousness, and to a balanced and integrated life. Light and dark are fundamental aspects of life. They are duality, essentially, yin and yang, feminine and masculine, and moon and sun. The latter pairing is the reason why this dualistic concept (duality, light and dark) is so important to be aware of. Our conscious minds are rooted in the light, they are the part of self and psyche we use to perceive, create opinions and beliefs, rationalize, analyze, think intuitively, and get by during the day. Of course, a lot of our conscious thoughts during the day are influenced by *subconscious* forces, in fact, a huge percentage of our conscious mind is rooted in subconscious influences. However, the main thing to know right now is that the conscious mind is associated with the daytime and sun. The *subconscious* is connected to the *moon* and *darkness*.

**Moon and Sun, yin and yang, darkness (shadow) and light are the fundamental philosophies of dreaming...**

Moon and Sun, yin and yang, darkness (shadow) and light are the fundamental philosophy of dreaming. Yin is dark, receptive, magnetic, feminine and corresponds to the Moon. Yang is light, active, dominant, masculine, and corresponds with the Sun. Dreaming is linked to lunar energies, the energy and influence of the moon and subconscious. Without being aware of the implications and applications of yin and yang, specifically the feminine and yin qualities & associations, it would be very hard to be able to interpret your dreams. This is due to the inherent and fundamental associations. Lunar yin energy, where Pisces sign thrives, is connected to the Shadow Self. The shadow self is your dark and repressed needs, wants, emotions and desires. The shadow self and personality is intrinsically associated with the subconscious, as your subconscious self is your "darkness." Both yin and the moon are *dark* in nature. Receptivity, magnetism, passivity and femininity... Regardless of whether you are man or woman, these 4 key qualities are essential to a balanced and healthy life. We live in an extroverted and masculine-oriented world (currently!), meaning that core feminine qualities, like receptivity, femininity and passivity, are repressed and even oppressed. Quite simply, we have become imbalanced, disconnected from the world of dreaming, feminine energy, and spiritual life.

We have yet to integrate our whole, unified and complete selves (on a collective level, although we are waking up). Life is a balance of light and dark, active and passive, and dominance & action and receptivity- of *surrendering* and *going with the flow*. Too much action and force results in the inability to surrender and be open to receive, therefore affecting the ability to dream. It's well known that many people in this day and age suffer from anxiety, insomnia, and poor sleep. Pisces as the most spiritually evolved sign aims to address this, they heal this issue with their core frequency which you will see later. Also, sensuality, sacred sexuality, and intuitive and instinctive gifts are tied into the subconscious and shadow. These are all predominantly feminine in nature and essence. Realigning with any one of these can help you develop self-awareness, compassion, unconditional love, and other beautiful & necessary qualities. Sex is sacred too, or should be. It's a sacred act connecting two hearts, minds, bodies and souls. But, when we're not in tune with our inner sensuality and divine feminine wisdom- which comes with a pure and strong heart and a sharpened intuition; we close ourselves off to spirit, inner divinity, and the sacredness of life. And, of course, to authentic & deep emotional bonds and intimate relationships.

Dreams send messages into our repressed desires, emotions and sensuality and sexuality. They show us how, where and why we're operating in specific ways, and they then assist us in changing to attain self-mastery. As for instincts and intuition, our intuition is the guiding force of light. It is our inner light and internal compass, so not being able to connect to subconscious and subtle energies, or the power and energy of the moon, makes us less likely to dream and receive the insight, wisdom and messages available. Too much masculine energy can lead to a neglect of certain energetic symbolism and imagery wishing to be shown. On the other hand, spiritual and deeply intuitive Pisces is aware of the imagery and symbolism in dreams, thus dreams with conscious awareness and openness to the magic of the universe. There is a reason why Shamanism, shamanic healing, and shamanic powers are linked with darkness and the subconscious, astral, and ethereal realms (dimensions, planes of consciousness). Shamans and shamanic practitioners recognize the power of the shadow realms and draw their knowledge, healing gifts and power from these spaces.

**We live in a masculine world. The moon and subconscious, i.e. the place we go in dreaming, are *feminine*. Feminine (lunar/yin) qualities include sensuality, sacredness, emotions, ancient wisdom, subtle energy and perception, receptivity, passivity, and instinctual and intuitive responses.**

# Chapter 1: PISCES

"Everybody is a genius. But if you judge a fish by its ability to climb a tree, it will live its whole life believing that it is stupid…"

~ Albert Einstein, *Pisces*

## Pisces Sign

Pisces is the 12th and final sign of the Zodiac born between February 19th and March 20th. Pisces is a water sign, Mutable (quality), ruled by Neptune, and with the astrological symbol of the two fish swimming in opposite directions. This represents Pisces' dual nature, how part of them is committed to transcending the physical limitations of the material plane and world, while the other seeks spiritual enlightenment, higher ideals and soul entwinement. On the one hand, Pisces is very grounded and connected to the earth, to the beautiful planet we reside in and the spirit of Gaia. They can achieve considerable success on the earth plane- in the material world- through creative and spiritual talents. On the other, Pisces doesn't care about worldly riches or material success; they are more concerned with universal themes of compassion, unconditional love, and making the world a better place. It's all about soul, spiritual alignment, and the power of their dreams. This is the "two fish swimming in opposite directions." Heaven and earth, spirit and matter, and divinity and the mundane.

The Pisces glyph is made up of two upright crescents facing opposite directions with a horizontal straight line in the middle. One crescent is the limited and physically restricted waking consciousness, i.e. non lucidity, 'real-world' matters and the material plane. While the other is a dreamlike "cosmic" consciousness, connected to the astral, ethereal-energetic, and spiritual planes. The line joining them is the bridge, or the bond, connecting and separating them simultaneously. This is why Pisces is able to swim in multiple directions, why they're so indecisive, and why they are so incredibly adaptable. Pisces has many gifts and talents because of their ruling symbol. Looking at the sign deeper, we can see that one fish swims towards Aries and the other to Aquarius (the two signs next to Pisces in the Zodiac). Spirit descending into matter is symbolic of Aries, being fully present and conscious in the world and connected to physical urges, instincts, and reality. The other is swimming upstream making its way to Source, the universe, and "home;" the soul. There's a sense of aloofness and detachment here as well, just like Aqaurius.

Pisces has many qualities and strengths. Being the final sign, this soulful and spiritually evolved being embodies traits and characteristics from *all* 12 star signs, which is rare. Pisces is the sign of unconditional love, universal compassion, empathy, and deep understanding and wisdom. Let's explore the main traits of Pisces now.

*Pisces Strengths*

### Sensitive ('the Empath')

Sensitive and very self-aware, Pisces is ruled by Neptune, the planet of dreams and the subconscious. This watery sign is able to tune into the feelings of everyone around them. They are so sensitive to the emotions, moods, impressions, thoughts and beliefs of others that it becomes sixth sense. Pisces sensitivity translates in two ways: firstly, it connects them to the subconscious mind and subtle forces, and spiritual awareness, insight and perception. Secondly, it means they are amazing friends and lovers! Being so sensitive allows them to care and nurture- provide for those they love. Sensitivity is a gift, not a curse. And this is one thing you should know with the Pisces sign. Some people see such extreme sensitivity as weakness; although it can lead to super- or hyper- sensitivity and downfall, which we explore in the Pisces Shadow, it is generally a strength. Pisces draws strength from the inner worlds, their feelings, impressions, psychic and intuitive insights, and advanced & evolved empathy.

Further, Pisces is the sign of "the empath." Empaths are extraordinary beings who can read minds, know *exactly* what it's like to be in another's shoes, and communicate telepathically. Subtly. Imagine dolphins speaking through supersonic waves, or snakes who sense vibrations through the air…. Pisces' skills are not too far apart from this.

## Spiritual (and Mystical)

Pisces is the most spiritual sign. Neptune is the planet of illusions, mysticism and spirituality. Being Pisces' ruler this implies a natural interest in and affinity with the occult, metaphysics, and esoteric fields. You will most likely find a typical Pisces with bohemian, colorful & flowy clothes, crystal and magical divination tools, and some profound piece of ancient wisdom to share. There is a *magical* quality about Pisces. They are so spiritual and connected to the unseen realms that they give off a dreamy and ethereal aura. Pisces is ultimately connected to the spiritual, astral and ethereal realms, multi-dimensionality too. Spiritual gifts are advanced and evolved, they may be telepathic, clairvoyant, claircognitive, clairsentient, clairaudient, and able to communicate with spirits or unseen entities and forces. Channeling and mediumship are associated with Pisces. Not only are they spiritual, but they're also *soulful*, they possess deep soul and depth; you won't find anyone as wise, spiritually evolved or enlightened as a Pisces. Their mind is attuned to another reality altogether and they can shift between dimensions, subtle planes of existence, with ease.

## A Dreamer, a Visionary

It's interesting that Pisces' dream symbol is "the Dreamer," because this sign *is* a dreamer. You will seldom to never discover a Pisces who isn't connected to their dreams. Being 'a dreamer' has two meanings. They are both visionaries and actual dreamers skilled in the realm of lucid dreaming, astral travel & projection, and receiving incredible guidance and insight from their dreams. With regards to the latter Pisces is able to enter dreamworlds and tune into subconscious and subtle insights. They may communicate (consciously) with dream characters or pick up on all the symbolism being shown. They don't need to read a book on how to do this, it comes instinctively to them. Being ruled by Neptune means they operate on a frequency of being deeply connected to this reality. Whereas others might have to spend years in training, or thousands of pounds or dollars on courses, workshops and 'lucid dreaming retreats,' or the like; it comes as effortlessly as dreaming to many people born into this sign. A Pisces knows there is an infinite sea of wisdom, inspiration, guidance and assistance available during sleep in the dreamworlds, and it is usually their playground! Linked here is the gift of precognition- precognitive dreaming. Their subconscious and spiritual vibration combined shows them something and- sometimes- it is a glimpse of the future. Alternatively, they will receive wisdom and information that will help a friend, family member or lover/partner, such as someone suffering with an ailment or injury and a dream character presenting the perfect herbal remedy or insight.

The other part of being a dreamer is being a visionary. Idealism is strong in this sign, as they're visionaries and stand for something higher, better, and more unified. They believe in "oneness" and interconnectedness, collective consciousness and rising above the everyday 'I' an ego reality. Pisces can work towards a better world quite easily. They have many dreams and silent powers linked to visionary gifts, yet they aren't always seen. Many Pisces choose to do their work "behind the scenes," meaning they're connected to some unseen or invisible reality only the Creator, Source, God or Spirit knows.

## Generous and Unconditionally Loving

Generosity doesn't come easily to everyone, but it does to this sign! As a sensitive and emotional, empathic, creature, Pisces is supremely giving. They will share their resources, joy, wisdom, love, home and hearth, abundance and positivity with everyone, and I mean *everyone*. Pisces will give their last coins to a homeless person and they'll do it with grace and modesty. They are generous with their time too. You can always count on Pisces sign listening to your problems or concerns, they're amazing listeners and great friends to have. Pisces is generally the soul sister or brother to everyone. This sign represents unconditional love. Universal love, unconditional love, unboundless compassion… There is a depth to Pisces that transcends (rises above) the issues and judgements of the earthly world. Pisces possess advanced levels of non-judgement, tolerance, and acceptance, both self-acceptance and acceptance for others. Pisces would still have compassion for a rapist or murderer. They see inside the depths and endless, infinite and eternal waters of the human nature and spirit.

Pisces recognizes how light and dark make up life, the universe itself, and how creation is an eternal battle (or dance and synergy?!) or light and dark, "good" and "evil," and yang and yin. Pisces understands and empathizes with the human condition, further being able to love someone 'warts and all.'

## Multi-talented, a Creative Genius

There is more to Pisces than meets the eye. Musical, artistic, creatively gifted and extraordinary, Pisces excels in a number of fields. In their youth, a Pisces child is generally shy and reserved. They appear quiet and ambitionless, yet inside their skin and mind there is a whole other reality altogether. Pisces is gifted with fine-tuned sensitivities and skills in perception. They can tune in to universal archetypes and subtle energy, they're blessed with an amazing mind and unique ways of perceiving things. They have many rare and original perspectives! Pisces tends to be a master of music, art, drawing, signing, and any other creative or artistic talent you can think of. They're *multi*-talented. People who don't know a Pisces are surprised at how brightly and powerfully this mystical water sign can shine, when they come out of their bubble. A bit of a jack of all trades and a master at many, Pisces is a magical, talented and musical creature. Poetry, writing, performing arts, and musical co-creation all come naturally to them; they can either be a silent but powerful background contributor, behind the scenes and contributing to the magic, ambience and groove or heartbeat of an act (performance, song, creation etc.), or in the limelight. Either way, this gentle soul is a force to be reckoned with.

### Imaginative

Expanding on, they're blessed with unique imaginative abilities. This is largely due to Neptune, their planetary ruler, however it also stems from their adaptable and open-minded nature. Pisces sign is deeply philosophical. Their mind is attuned with a higher, divine, cosmic and spiritual reality. Imagination pours through here. Visionary and abstract skills combine with keen insight and observation, and ability to use intuition with logic and reason. Pisces often draws from a vast reservoir of wisdom and knowledge acquired, and they use this to produce incredible creations or imaginative insights. Connected to this is the fact that they are unique *story-tellers*. They can wow you with mesmerizing poetry, spoken word, or enticing stories that remind you of the magic and unity of the universe. The three qualities of inspiration, vision and insight are well developed. The pisces ability to inspire others, raise humanity's vibration, and show you the power of the human spirit and imagination can be other-worldly- people recognize the divinity of this spiritual and soulful sign through their imaginative and visionary gifts.

### Adaptable

Being a *mutable* sign signifies a well-developed level of adaptability. Pisces is a bit of a chameleon, in truth. In addition to all of their spiritual, imaginative, creative, kind, and unconditionally loving gifts, Pisces possesses the charm and grace of a social butterfly. This usually introspective sign can be breathtakingly assertive and extroverted when they need to be. They can alternate between quiet and reflective to talkative and extremely witty. Pisces is chameleon-like in the sense that they can adapt to the current mood and environment. They read (suss out) the vibe and act accordingly. Sometimes they will be contemplative and only speak or interact when offering advice and sound wisdom, or empathy and emotional support, spiritual guidance or inspirational insight, other times they will appear as the life and soul of the party. Pisces is an all-rounder. Being so flexible allows them to thrive, shine and succeed and keep their peace- in a number of different social situations. Remember that as the 12th sign they embody traits and qualities from all previous 11 signs before.

So, in addition to all the strengths shared here, Pisces also has:-

- Aries' self-leadership and courage to fight for the underdog or what they believe is right.
- Taurus' determined, down-to-earth and chilled nature, and their fine-tuned senses (& love of sensuality!).
- Gemini's communication powers and ability to express themselves artistically and persuasively.
- Cancer's powerful instincts, emotional intelligence, and advanced imagination.
- Leo's love of creative self-expression and taking the spotlight (to inspire, educate or uplift others).
- Virgo's sense of service and helpfulness, and sweet and kind nature.
- Libra's diplomatic, justice-seeking, and harmonious nature... also, being an incredible listener.
- Scorpio's intensity and passion for spirituality, metaphysics, esotericism and self-mastery.
- Sagittarius' free-spirited travel loving vibe. Many Pisces are nomads and free spirits!
- Capricorn's humility and modesty combined with silent and subtle, yet powerful ambition.
- Aquarius' altruistic, humanitarian, and idealistic nature...

**Intuitive**

Pisces is also the most intuitive star sign. They're connected to an internal golden compass, an inner guiding light that tells them exactly what they need to know. And they can use this gift for self and for others. They know what path to take, when to talk, what to say- at the perfect time, and what choices are best in alignment with their soul and higher self, their best life. For others they use their intuitive gifts to offer wise counsel, sage advice and wisdom, and to be an incredible listener. Intuition births counsel. Pisces inevitably has the wisdom of a sage, someone evolved and advanced beyond their years. Intuition can be seen as a guiding light that leads the way, into the light and out of darkness, out of danger and into success. Such a strong intuition amplifies other hidden powers and abilities within (like the ones explored next). Whilst some people may need concrete facts and figures, Pisces has their own secret voice within. It is also where they draw much of their strength. They're blessed with inner knowing and powerful gut feelings. Of course, linked to this are well developed *instincts*. Pisces sign is wonderfully instinctive and connected to bodily feelings, messages and sensations. Once they reach a certain level of age and maturity they trust themselves impeccably, knowing that their gut feelings and internal responses don't lie.

**Seer-like, Psychic, Clairvoyant, Telepathic...**

Pisces has the sage-like wisdom and awareness of a seer. They're psychic and clairvoyant with some level of telepathic ability, telepathy of course being the gift to communicate without the need for words. This is linked to being an empath, or at the very least being very empathic. A Pisces will tune into cosmic sources of information and divinity. They will read between the lines, see beyond the veil, and use killer instincts combined with 'higher' seeing to get to the truth of matters. You can't hide anything from an on point Pisces... Liars, manipulative people, energy vampires, narcissists and toxic characters don't do well with this sign, Pisces sees right through illusion and hidden motives. Deception is a red flag and the Pisces mind is aligned with truth. This is truly one of the most psychic and naturally telepathic signs. As you will see in 'Pisces Careers,' they thrive in any spiritual or healing field.

### Intelligent

Many people underestimate this spiritual soul. Yes, it does look like mystical Pisces can float away with the fairies at any given moment, but they are ultimately incredibly intelligent. They are gifted with fine-tuned skills of observation and perception- they know what is going on. Silence is a superpower. They don't need to shout or be loud to be heard. Instead, they prefer to observe silently and find solace in the unseen, subconscious realms, and then share their wisdom when it is needed. This sign is very wise. Not only are they intuitive and draw their wisdom from the infinite source of creation- the spiritual and divine realms, but they also possess key cognitive abilities. Pisces can be analytical, logical, and problem-solving when they want to be. They love books, reading, educational podcasts and documentaries, and expanding their knowledge basis. If they don't choose a creative, healing or spiritual path most Pisces end up teaching or become a master of philosophy, or some specialist subject. There is a fabulous saying by Albert Einstein, also a Pisces, that fits here: "*If you judge a fish by its ability to climb a tree, it will live its whole life believing that it is stupid!*" Pisces knows their strengths and plays to them.

### Healing Gifts & Presence

Have you heard of someone having a *healing presence*? Or *healing hands*? Pisces has both of these. People change just through being near a pisces. Their presence is so powerful that great shifts are initiated, they can change people's energy field or aura through their own frequency (vibration) alone. They have a rare ability to uplift individual and collective (humanity's) consciousness and vibration through their power, presence, thoughts and inner being. Pisces represents soul, depth of spirit, and idealism. Their nature is catalytic! It is no wonder they are the 12th sign and the old souls of the Zodiac. Physically many Pisces are gifted with healing abilities. Life force energy flows through their hands and skills acquired in healing systems or arts such as Reiki, shamanic energy healing, and chakra and aura healing come naturally. Again, it is part of their core programming and energetic blueprint frequency. An eye gaze or look is another to create ripples and healing energy & light can be developed quite effortlessly.

### Selfless and Divine

Finally, Pisces is one of the most selfless signs. This is a watery trait, and is shared by the other sensitive-emotional-watery sign of the Zodiac: Cancer. The Pisces compassion knows no bounds. They are unconditional love personified, it's been established that they are supremely kind and generous; well, they're also selfless to the point of self-sacrifice. This has its highs and its lows which we explore next. Positively, the Pisces strength can be quite admirable. They draw their strength from their ability to put others' needs before their own. And this isn't just referring to humans! Some Pisces won't kill a mosquito due to the love and compassion they have for all sentient creatures. If it's living, breathing and moving, it's equal to this humble sign. That's another main quality Pisces possess: *humility*. Being so self-less (selfless aka 'self'-less) signifies evolved humility, grace and modesty. Pisces is able to transcend physical reality and the material world, and merge with the divine. Divine wisdom and inspiration flows to them because their higher self and higher consciousness energy channels are open. Their mind and higher self is merged with a different, more encompassing, (and holistic) reality. Once again, they are the 'Old Souls' of the Zodiac...

*Pisces Shadow*

**Self-Sacrificing**

Despite all their wonderful traits and strengths, Pisces can be very self-sacrificing. They sacrifice their own needs to help others. They actually put themselves down to 'raise others up,' and although this may seem like something positive and beautiful it actually leads to their downfall. A true Pisces can suffer and struggle throughout life, severely. One completely disregards their needs, emotions, feelings and psychological, emotional, physical and spiritual needs; all in the name of "service," or "kindness" and "compassion." This is the only sign to show the phenomena known as *idiot compassion*. Being compassionate to the point of idiocracy, ludicrousy even. Personal needs, aspirations, dreams and well-being can suffer as a result. Many problems arise through Pisces' self-sacrificing nature and virtually all of the remaining shadow traits below arise from this one character flaw. In the selfish VS selfless balance, Pisces takes things too far. Similar to water sign Cancer they can retreat into a shell if this is left unchecked. In childhood and youth they can suffer with mild or more extreme isolation or depression if they don't get the care, empathy and emotional support needed. And, such an extreme non-judgemental attitude can result in condoning anti-social or even 'evil' behavior.

**Moody & Withdrawn**

They can also be unbelievably moody. Reserved, shy and withdrawn, mild depression often takes over, and they don't know it! There is a natural and organic melancholy to pisces. They're hopeless romantics, very dreamy and connected to the subtle and subconscious realms too. Well, these dimensions are associated with "darkness"- and darkness is the opposite of *lightness*. Pisces can become deeply withdrawn within themselves, disconnected from society and the outside world, and give in to minor or extreme bouts of *isolation*. Pisces need to be careful of taking being a "lone wolf" too far to its negative extreme. In their pursuit of some romantic, artistic, or spiritual goal and ideal they become completely cut off from the outside world. Isolation gives rise to their fears and insecurities as well. Their empath nature makes them feel things so deeply and intensely that they forget to take care of their own needs, thus becoming moody and withdrawn. It can be difficult for them to function around fiery or masculine signs, like Aries, Leo and Sagittarius (fire) and Gemini, Libra and Aquarius (air). In their youth, they don't realize what is happening either- they're unaware of the impact such insensitivity has on their emotional, psychological, and spiritual wellbeing.

**Overly Emotional**

Pisces is very, very emotional. When they're in tune with their best self, they are able to channel their emotional intelligence and empathy into helping others. Yet, like a yoyo their emotions can hit a downward spiral which leads them into despair and suffering. Pisces feels the suffering of everything and everyone, every sentient creature from the tiniest bug to the largest mammal, and the earth and planet itself. So, they take on that pain and suffering and further absorb it. This isn't healthy. It can leave a super sensitive Pisces feeling distraught and suffering in silence, ultimately taking on the pain and wounds of everyone around them. Or the entire planet (and cosmos) as a whole. Pisces functions at a higher and more evolved emotional frequency than most, virtually everyone (fellow water signs Cancer and Scorpio come very close). It is a core part of their nature and is inescapable. Being so sensitive and empathic can lead to issues in self-worth and self-esteem, reduced confidence and a lack of discernment. There is a desire to people-please and appease, to please everyone through taking on the role of the empath and counselor.

**Escapist**

And being so super, hyper and overly emotional (and sensitive) leads to their other shadow tendency: escapism. Pisces are master escapists. They can create fantasy worlds and go so far into themselves that they lose touch of reality altogether. They may become lost in drugs, sex, lust, t.v. or technology. Pisces has an *addictive personality* when at their lowest. Addictions feature strongly in a young and less evolved Pisces' life. This sign feels safe in the inner worlds they've created, so escapes from the cold and harsh conditions of reality. Be mindful of how sensitive this sign is. They are so compassionate and caring that the gravitation towards escapism stems from feeling too much, too deeply. The other main cause is a lack of responsibility- a lack of grounding. Practical reality, responsibilities and duties in addition to physical needs and self-care, can often be overlooked and rejected altogether. And, they're illusion and fantasy prone. Being ruled by planet Neptunes signifies a capacity for giving into illusions, or becoming lost in them. It can be hard for Pisces to separate truth and reality from fantasy and fiction.

**Ungrounded, Impractical**

Continuing on… Pisces prefers to be connected to some spiritual or divine (or creative/artistic/imaginative) reality. This sign neglects their physical body and focuses solely on spirit and the soul, or gifts and talents linked to the subtle and ethereal realms. A key lesson throughout life is for Pisces to learn that they have a body, and it's important to nourish it! Secondly, practical responsibilities including finances are overlooked. Pisces can be a sucker for a sob story- they're prone to being conned or played for a fool. Being so impractical leads to disconnection on multiple levels. For someone so connected and in tune with themselves and the world around, a lack of groundedness can have strong contrary effects. Bank statements, bills and payments are left unchecked, health issues go unhealed, and disaster and financial danger can loom around the corner. Their intentions are pure, it's just practicalities aren't their strength, unfortunately.

**Victim-Martyr-Savior Complex!**

Pisces is known for someone called the victim, martyr & savior complex. This means, they alternate between victim (actual or playing), martyr, and savior. They try to save everyone else and be the hero or heroin while setting themselves up for personal failure, ultimately leading them to victimhood. Vice versa. This complex is birthed from trying to do good, from being *the dreamer* of the Zodiac. Being so idealistic has its shortcomings. Even when they are genuinely a victim (it is a cold and harsh world, after all…) Pisces needs to learn to take responsibility and own up to their role. This will help to bring back their personal power. 'Let the haters hate,' also- there's no need to try and heal or change everyone. Sometimes, a sensitive and sweet Pisces will encounter energy vampires or narcissistic people. The victim-martyr-savior complex shadow trait suggests that they must look past the "oneness" philosophy they believe in, and recognize separation and individual consciousness.

**'A beautiful fool…'**

Overly-trusting, Pisces is clearly the fool of the Zodiac. This sign *lacks boundaries*, 'where does self start and end?' 'Who's thoughts and feelings are these?' 'Do these belong to me?' Pisces has the ability to merge with the transcendental, as you're now aware, but this leaves them open to psychic attack, negative, and toxic energy. Or simply the false judgements and projections of others. Even when Pisces isn't unconsciously absorbing everyone's harsh and usually untrue judgements and harmful projections, they still pick up on everyone's "stuff." Stuff being beliefs, opinions, inner wounds, pain, emotions, impressions, reflections and follies. Anything & everything a person holds Pisces can pick up on. When they absorb this, it leads to a number of problems; they become the fool, everyone's verbal or ethereal punchbag and are subsequently used and/or abused. People tend to take advantage of Pisces' kind & giving nature. Selflessness is a target for selfish, narcissistic, characters, so *energy depletion* (being drained!) is another thing they have to watch out for. Overall, having such weak boundaries can lead to a lack of discernment, naivety, and many problems. A genuine but gullible Pisces can be played for a fool, connected out of large sums of money, or their love and heart, and used- taken advantage of.

*Pisces are the most sensitive, dreamy, compassionate and empathic sign of the Zodiac. They can often communicate subtly and instinctively with animals, plants, and nature. A Pisces' sensitivity and instinctive need to nurture, care for others, and protect knows no bounds…*

**Why know about the Pisces Strengths and Shadow traits?**

As you will see in the next chapter, a person's character, strengths, flaws & follies define (and shape) who someone is. Dream and waking worlds are interlinked… in waking life time, we tend to use our conscious minds. But, our subconscious mind is very close to us- it's just below the surface and in some signs (like the water signs) it is more easily accessed. It's readily accessible. Knowing the ins and outs of a person's true character can help you to understand how and why they function the way they do in dreams. Each specific strength and flaw influences, shapes and creates the type of dreams we have, the themes and messages conveyed, etc. and our susceptibility to lucid dreaming or dream manifestation.

In Pisces' case, we are actually **The Dreamer**, the only sign with this dream symbol and the only sign ruled by the planet Neptune; the planet of dreams, spirituality, mysticism and the subconscious mind. Thus, a Pisces dreams will be very different to, say, an earth or fire sign! In other words, you wouldn't be able to discover your dreaming patterns, omens, and key themes without knowing what makes you, 'you.'

## Pisces In Love

Pisces is a romantic at heart. They are lovers, not fighters. They love poetry, music, candles, sensuality, mysticism and soulbonds. Soulmates are an integral part of a Pisces' life, they believe wholeheartedly in soulmate connections and are ideally looking for a mind, body & spirit connection. Pisces loves to love. There is a dreamy and ethereal quality about a Pisces' love style, however this doesn't mean they aren't wild. Pisces is a dual sign in nature. On the one hand they are sensual and spiritual, gentle and devoted- just like the strengths shared above suggest. But, on the other hand, they are prone to wanderlust and wild displays of love and affection. Pisces can be a very kinky and liberated lover when they feel comfortable! This is the key though, they need to feel comfortable. Safety, security and emotional connection are extremely important to them. Sweet and sensual or at one with their inner animal, the 'chameleon adaptability' mentioned earlier works in their favor.

Pisces sign is turned off by violence, cruelty, and coldness of *any* type. If you don't honor, cherish and respect their emotional sensitivity and need for deep, authentic bonding, they simply don't want or need you. This is very different to, say, bold and fiery Aries (fire) and frivolous & flirty Sagittarius (fire), or cerebral and mental Gemini (air). Below we briefly explore compatibility. In saying this, Pisces can be surprisingly submissive, although it's not much of a surprise when we see their personality traits. They are happy to be dominated (with consent) or to dominate. Their submissive side comes out when they feel seen, valued and appreciated. Furthermore, they are *incredibly* passionate. They bring passion and inspiration into their love life and let it shine in more intimate ways, and on a platonic level. Remember that Pisces is a feminine sign. In love, they can be receptive, magnetic, devoted, pleasing, intuitive, instinctive and subconsciously connected. When evolved and connected to their higher self and adult body this partner is incredibly magnetic and loving, an ideal lover and partner. Being such an incurable romantic has its downfalls when young or not fully healed (wounds, ancestral and family trauma, cosmic/universal trauma, etc.), however. Pisces can become infatuated and give into flights of serious fancy. They always have their eyes on a lover and potential soulmate or two (or three, four, five...) and fantasize a lot. Fantasy takes over and dreams and daydreaming become overpowered by vivid fantasies and soul-melting scenarios of ideal love.

Sweet Pisces is loyal, faithful and devoted. They're generous and compassionate in love, creative and imaginative too. They enjoy sharing their artistic gifts and unique imagination within a relationship. They want a lover with similar values- someone who is compatible, and a person with well developed spiritual beliefs and philosophies. They don't care so much if you have *exactly* the same beliefs, they just want you to have some. Knowing yourself is important. Most importantly, you need to be kind, gentle, soulful and with something extra about you, like some talent or gift, strength or ability that sets you apart from the rest. Intuition combined with a unique instinct allows them to navigate the ins and outs of their relationship. They can see into their lover's soul, mind, heart and innermost needs and desires; Pisces is a gem to have as a partner.

One thing to note… Pisces hates rejection. They can't handle it, in fact. For someone with such great inner strength and spiritual devotion they become weak and extremely sad when they're rejected. This is because Pisces takes rejection personally, failing to recognize it is a reflection of the other person. Pisces is a *universal mirror*. They represent unconditional love and universal compassion, and their lover gets the same treatment; they are unselfish (selfless) lovers who could happily spend a lifetime pleasing and showering someone special in gifts and love. Fantasy and mystery are strong too. Many Pisces are fantasy lovers, happy to act out your desires and roleplay scenarios. Alternatively they may create love affairs and fantasy scenes inside their mind- a Pisces can achieve more pleasure going solo with their own vivid imagination and spirit than being with the wrong person. Furthermore, this sign is prone to tantric sex, soul union on the highest vibration. In other words sex is a spiritual and soulful experience. They want to merge with another on *every* level and feel the ecstasy and bliss of making love with their mind, body, heart, emotional self and soul.

Want to win a Pisces' heart? Read them the poetry of Rumi while massaging their feet, or dedicate some part of your heart and life to helping animals or the planet. Charity, humanitarianism and eco-care (environmentalism) are turn-ons! Pisces can be irresistible. They protect a dreamy aura and usually have large, hypnotizing eyes. People get lost in a Pisces' eyes… Be mindful, sex and emotions are entwined- one and the same, to a Pisces. You won't be able to get to their body unless you've touched their heart, spirit and emotional body in some way. Commitment is a possibility however a younger Pisces is prone to wanderlust, love affairs and flings, and a certain level of frivolity. This sign can be quite hard to pin down, and they often have many admirers. Later in life they are able to be faithful and loyal. *But*, it should be noted that many people born into this sign are open to more tribal and polyamorous displays of love and sexual union. It is not uncommon to find a Pisces as part of a loving, sensitive, and spiritually open 3-way partnership, or "experimenting" in a tantric and yogic community. You should be aware that this sign is not jealous at all. Although they seek emotional depth and can't experience love without intimacy they provide a lot of independence and freedom to their lovers. Jealousy isn't for them and it's not uncommon to have multiple partners or live in tantric and polyamorous communities, where love is free.

Pisces is a magical creature. Anyone who has been with a spiritually mature and evolved Pisces can tell you that unconditional love is real. This imaginative, gifted, sensitive and intuitive water sign will take you to the depths of your soul, raise you up into your own greatness and divinity, and keep you high and mighty. Sometimes they will stay with you there and at other times they will leave you, always blessing you with pearls of wisdom and divine inspiration along your journey. Pisces selflessness' reflects into their approach to love and romance too. Mystery, depth, and the vast beauty of the ocean defines a Pisces.

Finally, it's important to know that, as a dual sign, you need to be very intuitive and connected to your instincts to be with a Pisces. Yes, they give you your freedom, they're prone to wanderlust and polyamory, multiple (conscious) lovers, and love their freedom and independence themselves, but they are still primarily emotional creatures. This gentle and sincere soul requires a lot of love and support. They will rarely ask for it- you should know how much they need and when to give it to them. This is the key to a successful and long-term relationship with a Pisces. Instinctive, attentive, caring and supremely kind, a Pisces will love you for eternity and with unconditional love and compassion. The worst thing you could do? Take advantage of their sweet and nurturing nature. Once they've suspected that your intentions aren't pure or that they have been played for a fool, or simply that they aren't valued, appreciated or wanted, they have no problem sending you love and wishing you well. This can be karmically wounding to people who haven't reached the same level of spiritual enlightenment as them! At the end and start of each day, it will always be about Soul for them. The rest comes afterwards.

## Pisces Compatibility

Earth and water are most compatible with Pisces. The earth signs blend well with the Piscean spirit. Taurus and Capricorn complement them and appreciate their emotional sensitivity, and Pisces likes the security and grounding earth provides. Taurus is the most compatible out of the earth signs. This is because Taurus is deeply romantic and ruled by Venus, Venus is exalted in Pisces. There is a mutual understanding and many shared passions, likes, and interests. Taurus is very sensual and down-to-earth with a chilled and relaxed persona- Pisces loves this! Also, Taurus sign is very much connected to Mother Earth and the energies of nature. This earth sign is romantic and intelligent, wise and gentle. Capricorn is another compatible one. Capricorn is modest and sensual too, so there is a harmony here. Virgo is Pisces opposite thus the sign with which Pisces can find most balance. Pisces can look to Virgo's love of order, duty and practicality to find grounding in their life. Simultaneously, Pisces teaches Virgo how to be more sensitive and emotionally vulnerable. Water compliments earth well and Pisces enjoys being a teacher and wayshower, inspiring change in usually overly-organized and inflexible Virgo. Pisces teaches Virgo how to broaden their horizons, expand their mind, and open up the spiritual-energetic, subtle universe.

The most compatible signs are the water ones. A Pisces-pisces pairing can be a match made in heaven. This romance is dreamy, deeply sensual, nurturing and compassionate. They understand each other and enjoy healing, spiritual and creative pathways together. But, there is a downfall to two 'dreamers' coming together. Pisces and Pisces can become extremely ungrounded and impractical, neglecting financial and practical duties altogether. There is a tendency to get lost in fantasy or dreamworlds, or give into the other shadow part of their personality: codependency. Mild toxic energy is possible. Cancer and Scorpio are magnetic and sparkling matches. Cancer is compassionate, highly instinctual, imaginative, empathic and sensitive. Pisces loves this. Truly soulmate potential here, true love too. Pisces and Cancer can adore each other and create a lot of extraordinary creations. They inspire each other and provide the other all the love and support they need. The only minor distortion is the fact that Cancer is slightly more sensitive and codependent than freedom-loving Pisces, therefore clinginess and some smothering love may be a problem. This can be overcome with healthy communication and honesty.

Scorpio is an amazing match- two star crossed lovers! Lots of love, passion, romance and intimacy define this partnership, with a significant focus on a shared sense of mission. Destiny, service, common interests and goals that can be combined to become a "power couple." Scorpio brings out Pisces ambitious and high-flying side while secretly being devoted to this intensely sexy Scorpion (Scorpio's ruling glyph). This couple can alternate between so attentively loving and romantic, gentle and caring to wild and steamy. They bounce off each other and feed one another's light and divinity in the process.

Fire and air signs are least compatible, but this doesn't mean harmony and happiness can't be achieved. It just takes some work. Aries, Leo and Sagittarius are fiery and insensitive, they tend to overpower and dominate poor Pisces. They tend to see some of the best Pisces' strengths as weaknesses too, which isn't a good sign. This can lead an already trusting and open Pisces to insecurity, self-doubt and low self-esteem. At the worst, Aries, Leo and Sagittarius can all diminish Pisces' light and source of personal power completely. It's often not conscious or intentional, it's just a major innate difference in character. Further, the fire signs don't give Pisces the love, care and delicate attention they need. Pisces often feels neglected or confused even, as if the relationship doesn't have the longevity they would like. On a positive note, there is incredible potential for immense creativity and imaginative inspiration, especially with Leo and Sagittarius. These are two of the most creative and artistically gifted star signs- alongside Cancer and Pisces, therefore Pisces can achieve a lot with these two. Creative inspiration, visionary goals, shared dreams and artistic projects can all get a powerful boost from a water-fire combo. Pisces feels inspired and empowered with them too. Of course, emotional and intuitive Pisces gives all three fire signs the 'level up' they need, showing them the true meaning of talent, inspiration and soul passions and gifts. This pushes them (Pisces) to be the best version of themselves and step into their role of creator, changemaker, and teacher or wayshower. Overall Pisces like the power and vitality, life force and excitement associated with Aries, Leo and Sagittarius.

Gemini, Libra and Aquarius prefer to connect on a mental and intellectual level, while Pisces seeks out emotional (and spiritual) bonding. So, there can be some problems here. This is actually the main fundamental 'flaw' with a Pisces-air relationship. Some positives… the air signs are all creative and imaginative, traits Pisces loves, of course. Because they are all mental, i.e. mind based, they let Pisces step into positions of leadership and self-assertion. Pisces becomes more open and self-expressive around the air signs, they feel able to express their ideas, intellect, thoughts and impressions. Simultaneously the air signs benefit from Pisces' dreamy, emotional and psychic-intuitive attributes. Gemini is the least compatible out of the bunch due to Gemini- the 'Twins'- being another sign of duality and ruled by Mercury. Mercury is all about thinking, Neptune symbolizes instincts and feelings. Gemini also tends to be disconnected from their emotions which is an issue. Libra, however, is ruled by Venus, the planet of love, beauty, sensuality and feminine sexuality. Venus is a feminine planet and Pisces is feminine, so there is mutual understanding and harmony. Libra is further represented by the symbol (astrological glyph) of the 'Scales;' diplomacy, compromise, fairness, equality, balance and harmony. Libra seeks peace and loves romance, sensual expression and intimacy and affection, just like soulful Pisces! Aquarius, the 'Water-bearer,' is an air sign but is watery in nature. Intuitive, imaginative, empathic, altruistic, humanitarian… There are lots of shared interests and opportunities for harmonious bonding.

So, to recap, the most compatible signs are Taurus, Cancer, Scorpio, Capricorn and Pisces. These all have major soulmates and true love potential. Virgo, Libra and Aquarius are middle on the compatibility scale, while Aries, Gemini, Leo and Sagittarius are least compatible.

## Pisces Careers

Pisces has many ideal career choices. Being so gifted and multi-talented means they would thrive in a number of fields. Let's break this down.

### 1. Spiritual, healing and metaphysical fields

Spiritual healing, becoming a Reiki Master teacher, Energy Worker or Shamanic healer/practitioner are all suited to Pisces. As a psychic, sensitive and spiritually gifted water sign, Pisces would thrive as a Tarot Reader, Astrologer, Metaphysical teacher, Seer, Clairvoyant, Medium (spiritual channeling), Priest, Spiritual Leader, or Healer of any type. Therapy, martial arts, yoga, holistic and complementary therapies, tantra and any esoteric, metaphysical or spiritual field are all ideal paths.

### 2. Caregiving and counseling fields

Social or support work, nursing, counseling, elderly companionship, caring (as a carer, home-care worker etc.) and charity, humanitarian and environmental fields are perfect career choices. Anything that makes use of Pisces' kind, caring, gentle and compassionate nature.

### 3. Creative and imaginative fields

Of course, Pisces shines and excels in the Arts. Being a musician, spoken word poet, speaker, soul singer, artist, painter, children's story-teller, writer, author, wordsmith, graphic designer, creative director, photographer, fashion designer or film director all come naturally to Pisces. Creativity and the imagination are key themes.

### 4. Entertainment, travel and hospitality

Because Pisces is so creative, philosophical and adaptable they also suit any role in entertainment, travel and tourism, and hospitality. Many Pisces choose to be world nomads and work online from their laptop. Freelancing is another ideal route. Also, volunteering on eco, animal or community projects. Pisces could happily leave the material world behind and go and live on a commune, or spend months to years on a work-exchange program where they receive free food & accommodation in exchange for work, and of course learning new skills. Pisces is prone to wanderlust and a traveling spirit vibe.

### 5. Self-employment and soul-preneur

Finally, being a soulpreneur, a soulful entrepreneur or self-employed in any skill or field is right on this fish's wavelength. Pisces like to be their own boss just as much as they're happy to cooperate in a team. The other side of this is a life and path of devotion, selfless service; working and living in an ashram or religious or spiritual community is just as interesting as being their own boss bringing in the dollar.

## Pisces In Platonic Relationships

Pisces is a gem of a friend, family member and business partner. They're caring and supportive with amazing listening skills. They use their intuition and balance it with sage wisdom and advice to produce remarkable results. Idealistic, deeply intelligent and visionary, Pisces can tune into the world of subtle energy for extraordinary creations and achievements. Being emotional and sensitive allows them to find similarities in the shared human spirit, which is something even the most stern or level-headed, apparently emotionless, person appreciates. Pisces has a gift of bringing out people's hearts and warmth. They connect to virtually everyone on an authentic and genuine level and are loved by many! Even in business and serious situations, a true Pisces can make you feel like you're at an all-embracing festival or kindred spirit gathering. Their eyes are entrancing. They stare at your core and soul and help you to break past illusion, fear and negativity.

Pisces are helpful and service oriented. They will always use their intuitive insight and wisdom to shine light on situations- they believe in self-mastery and being the best version of yourself. Pisces aims to *inspire*. They will use their love, wisdom, awareness and subtle-spiritual perception to assist family members or bosses. They are brave and fearless for a just and righteous cause, and for sticking up for the underdog. Never question a Pisces' integrity and spiritual grace, however, as you may see a very different side to this sensitive and humble creature. Surprisingly, Pisces has a very passionate and fiery side that comes up as fierce protection and magnetism that shocks and awes. Even when they're standing their ground or raising their voice (which is very rare) it is done with a certain magic and as a force of compassion. Neptune's influence gives them a rare spiritual power that speaks to the depths of one's soul. They're not afraid of darkness either, and this can lead to genius creations in the artistic and creative worlds. As a work colleague or business partner, they are helpful and compromisable yet know how to take charge. Teamwork, unity consciousness and harmony are very important to them, however they don't like being undermined or undervalued either. A secret part of them wants to be seen, heard and understood- recognized for their gifts and intelligence. They may not show it but Pisces can want to be seen as the star they are.

Mostly, they are inspiring, humble and modest. They possess a chilled and relaxed, friendly aura and vibe. Stress, worry and irrational or illusionary fears don't work for them. They're committed to truth and justice as well, a higher reality. Spiritual harmony, philosophy and idealistic projects are integral to a Pisces' path... Because of their dual nature they can be up in the clouds, with their mind set on big goals and visionary dreams, or down-to-earth and humble. When they're less concerned with their dreams and aspirations you will find a Pisces helping friends, family and loved ones with their empathy and care. Devotion defines this sensitive and mystical creature. Sometimes, they don't even need to say anything- they can simply *be* around you and make you feel at ease, peaceful, or relaxed. Remember that Pisces has a powerful healing presence and spirit. A self-assured and strong Pisces has mastered the art of being; they actively change mindsets, moods, environments and social energy through their advanced emotional, psychological and spiritual frequency alone. At this highest level, this manifests on a physical level so they step fully into their power and evolved vibration, further enabling them to be a real force of change and global, or collective, awakening.

Finally, Pisces sign is a natural counselor and nurturer even in a business or very professional setting. They may be sitting on a park bench and have a stranger come up to them and unload all their problems. People feel safe around Pisces. Being an empath signifies that they welcome people in need of healing. Their aura says, *'I'm happy to listen to you and hold space for you. I am pure love and acceptance, compassion and non-judgement.'* It's an amazing gift to possess. The only negative with Pisces in platonic relationships is how they can be walked over, taken for granted, and used. Issues in boundaries and discernment are common, so you should always be mindful of how genuine and sensitive this soulful sign is. Some people tend to use Pisces as their emotional dumping ground! At the worst, as was briefly mentioned in 'Pisces Shadow,' they can be conned or played for a fool. Naivety and being open to the manipulations of others are one of their worst character traits.

Loyal, devoted, gentle and impressionable, Pisces is a superstar! A force to be reckoned with. Putting others' needs before their own doesn't take away from their personal goals and aspirations. Pisces possess silent ambitions, subtle power, and an incredibly advanced spirit. People-pleasing may be frequent, but they always return back to their own source of power and inspiration. And inspirational is what this divine and multi-talented person is. Passionate and expressive, selfless and with an extraordinary imagination (and *many* creative gifts & talents); Pisces can show you to waters of divinity and the depths of your soul. They can do so with pure poetry, mesmerizing storytelling, or musicianship that verges on magician-ship. Emotional intelligence and empathy are more advanced in Pisces than any other sign, and they're accepting, tolerant, wise and faithful.

### *Famous Pisces?*

Some famous Pisces include Albert Einstein, Edgar Cayce, Dakota Fanning, Antonio Vivaldi, Rudolph Steiner, Rihanna, George Harrison, Quincy Jones, Immortal Technique, Erykah Badu, Nina Simone, Wanda Sykes, Michelangelo, Victor Hugo, Smokey Robinson, Queen Latifah, Seal, Corinne Bailey Rae, Steve Jobs, James Redfield, Linus Pauling, Sidney Poitier, George Friedrich Handel, Kenneth Grahame, Benji and Joel Madden, Drew Barrymore, Boris Kodjoe, Yuri Gagarin, Rachel Weisz, Ansel Elgort, Alexander G. Bell, Douglas Adams, Justin Bieber, George Washington, Mikhail Gorbachev, Jon Bon Jovi, Eva Longoria, Frederic Chopin, L. Ron Hubbard, Simone Biles, Vanessa Williams, Liza Minnelli, Valentina Tereshkova, Ellen Terry, Kurt Cobain, and Adam Levine.

*Interesting fact*: Albert Einstein shares the same birthdate as the author, Grace Gabriella Puskas (March 14th).

# Chapter 2: PISCES AND DREAMS

"Once upon a time, I... dreamt I was a butterfly, fluttering hither and thither, to all intents and purposes a butterfly. I was conscious only of my happiness as a butterfly, unaware that I was Chou. Soon I awaked, and there I was, veritably myself again."

~ Lao Tzu

## The Dreaming Patterns of Pisces

Firstly, Pisces *loves* to sleep. Pisces can sleep for hours, so much so that some people might consider them lazy. But, the thing to know about Pisces is that sleep and dreaming is a way to spiritually recharge. It is a route back to their true self, back to self-alignment and healing, and back to their spiritual source of power. Pisces merges with Source and Spirit, the divine, when they dream. Even when it appears to be a deeply symbolic dream where their subconscious is highly active they are still getting the healing they need. Subconscious dreams rich with wisdom and insight provide peace and clarity in waking life, so their subconscious gets a recharge and reboost. They can also use dreaming as a way to cut distractions or negative energy from the outside world. Toxic energy is very harmful to them therefore sleep is a powerful route to wholeness. Mental/psychological, emotional, physical and spiritual healing is achieved through sleep... And a Pisces can dream at *any* time of day.

This means being a night owl doesn't affect their dreaming habits. Of course, it is best to sleep and dream at night, when the Moon and night time's energies are strongest, but mystical and spiritual Pisces is still able to out-dream every other Zodiac sign. Pisces is intelligent, intuitive, and gifted perceptively. They see dreams as a way to receive wisdom from their subconscious mind, and to access unseen knowledge and subtle power. Dreams are viewed as meaningful riddles and mazes- just as they should be.

**Pisces is intelligent, intuitive, and gifted perceptively. They see dreams as a way to receive wisdom from their subconscious mind, and to access unseen knowledge and subtle power...**

So, Pisces is the ultimate dreamer. Their planetary ruler Neptune is the planet representing dreams, illusion and mysticism, in addition to imagination and the subconscious mind. Sleep should be seen as an elongated meditation or spiritual healing session for a Pisces. It's a chance to rejuvenate themselves, refresh their minds, and overcome any prominent shadow tendencies, fears or illusions that have taken over in waking life. It's easy for a Pisces to pick up on other people's "stuff," aka, to absorb the judgements, illusions, ill-intentions or suffering and pain of others, which manifests as Pisces acting as a constant healer or counselor and therapist!

There's another Pisces dreaming pattern it may be useful to be aware of. This is for those Pisces who don't conform to the structures of society, traditional '9 to 5s' or simply have lots of free time. This is the pattern of taking regular sleeping breaks, such as 2- 3 hours throughout the day and night. Despite being simple looking, i.e. uninteresting and idle or ambitionless, the pisces spirit is rich with endless things to learn, embody and accomplish. This means they love to fill their days with skill mastery, wisdom acquisition, and a range of projects, hobbies and talents. Some Pisces literally have 1 hundred things going on, yet no one would know. They can be very secretive and private. Thus, some Pisces choose to alternate between dream and waking worlds effortlessly and frequently. Between naps or sleep breaks they study, read, exercise, master languages and musical instruments, write, journal and give the mind, emotions, body and spirit a workout. Then they go into dreamspace to supercharge their subconscious, and receive wisdom and downloads from the dream reality.

Oh, this is another thing: Pisces sign receives *downloads*. Yes, you heard correctly. They are able to plug into the divine and be a transmitter and receive of cosmic consciousness, spiritual ideals, and divine inspiration. We did say Pisces is *extra*ordinary. Furthermore, Pisces is an avid lucid dreamer also known for evolved gifts in astral travel and astral projection. Intuition and psychic gifts get heightened during sleep and vice versa (intuitive and psychic gifts allow this sign to dream lots). Pisces dreams are vivid. They're full of imagery and useful symbolism which provides insight into their emotions, beliefs, health, well-being and current life themes and patterns. A Pisces can go to sleep unsure of something, such as an issue in love, romance, career or health and spirituality, and then wake up with 110% surety. Dreams are tools for them, tools to healing, wisdom and guidance. Many pisces keep dream journals or diaries and record their dreams for future self-discovery. They like to see into the past, present, and future and keep their self-awareness levels high. *Knowledge is power*. A true Pisces will further use the wisdom and insight from their dreams and seek to assist others, or preach a little. Fortunately, many people know that Pisces are *the* people to tune to for knowledge on their dreams and dreaming in general. So "preaching" is justifiable seen as "teaching," or even a kind and generous offering of specialist skills.

Pisces has a wild imagination and dreamy gaze... When they go to sleep, they enter dream space attuned to a certain "frequency." Everyone has a unique vibration and overall set of characteristics and vibrational qualities that make them the whole person they are. With Pisces, the sensitive and mystical, empathic and super selfless water sign, they are able to enter a dream quite quickly. It can be as effortless as breathing for those Pisceans who have mastered certain advanced dreaming techniques, like lucid dreaming, shamanic dreaming, astral travel or astral projection. There are multiple levels to a Pisces' dreaming patterns. For others, such as Aries who can only see imagery and symbols or Sagittarius who is equally less "prophetic" and precognitive, there is less choice. There's less multidimensionality and few dream realms available. Pisces has access to the whole scope, the vastness of the human consciousness, and the divine one (consciousness). *What does this mean?* It signifies dreaming patterns themselves will be quite eclectic. Depending on which phase, state of mind and emotion, and evolutionary cycle Pisces is in they will go through altered states of consciousness, affecting their dream themes, symbols & patterns. The best way to understand this is through the various dream themes and signs shared in remaining chapters.

Ultimately, Pisces sign is expansive with the ability to merge with the infinite. They are boundless and all-encompassing and frequently go through regular patterns of processing, learning, integration and releasing until certain cycles and pieces of wisdom (such as a personal or universal teaching) have been integrated. Pisces are masters of surrendering to the evolutionary cycle and stages of development, absorbing wisdom and lessons- regardless of how tricky they may be, and then letting go (of things that longer serve them or their higher self) or embodying the qualities wishing to be grounded into their physical being.

## 'The Dreamer' (Pisces Dream Symbol)

To put this into perspective, below are the dream symbols of all 12 star signs:

- Aries: *The Passionate*
- Taurus: *The Bastion*
- Gemini: *The Creator*
- Cancer: *The Distortion*
- Leo: *The Leader*
- Virgo: *The Mentalist*
- Libra: *The Control*
- Scorpio: *The Illuminated*
- Sagittarius: *The Explorer*
- Capricorn: *The Fortress*
- Aquarius: *The Smith*
- Pisces: *The Dreamer*

As you can see, Pisces sign is the *only* zodiac sign to embody the Dreamer. As this is a book and exploration on dreams I would say this is pretty significant. Their dream symbol can be seen to be reflected in some of the positive qualities shared earlier. Impressionable, adaptable, instinctive and psychic; intuitive, chameleon-like, compassionate and possessing advanced empathy, this fish knows how to swim and find shorelines within dreams. They're comfortable with all aspects of the dream worlds because they are *the dreamer*. Neptune has unique symbolism that assists them too. It is worth knowing, especially if you yourself are a Pisces.

## Neptune's Symbolism & Associations

Neptune is known as the 'God of the Sea.' This large planet has links to (rules) spirituality, the Arts, creativity, inspiration, mysticism, dreams, psychic gifts, and illusion. Supernatural and extrasensory phenomena and gifts also come under Neptune's reign. Entertainment industries, film and media, and all forms of creative trade are included; writing, publishing, illustration, poetry, music and art…. This is why Pisces is often gifted in public speaking, performing, and entertaining through a number of crafts (drama, acting, spoken word, story-telling, music performance, etc). Craftsmanship too. This planet has a youthful and soulful energy about it, although it can sometimes be naive. Alongside the *innocence* and naivety is a deep wisdom and self-awareness. Pisces is a bit of an enigma. This telepathic and sensitive water sign is the 12th sign also known as the 'Old Souls' of the Zodiac, so they are the perfect representation of Neptune energy.

Neptune's influence allows Pisces to be instinctual. They're able to rely on their evolved empathy & intuition to navigate life's waters. This planet requires a spiritual or soul connection... Kindred spirits, soulmate bonds, and true love are often associated with this planet and further the Pisces sign. They seek depth. Secondly, idealism and visions come under its influence. Visionary qualities like the gift of foresight and more psychic abilities such as precognitive vision, the ability to 'precognitive dream,' and tune into universal archetypes and subconscious imagery and wisdom are included. Neptune allows one to connect to the subconscious waters and vast landscapes of the imagination, multidimensionality, and spiritual and mystical *transcendental* awareness. Pisces merges with the divine with Neptune's assistance. On a positive, wisdom and a sage-like energy is available. When expressed negatively there can be some immaturity, spaciness, illusion and confusion. The other side of the coin with spirituality & mysticism is illusion which brings distortion in levels of thinking and rationalizing. Logic and reason tend to be lost with ungrounded Pisces.

Alternatively getting lost in dreamworlds or a purely spiritual way of seeing things can take over. Effects of this negative Neptune placement include an inability to separate reality from fantasy. There is an over-emphasis on mystical and/or artistic values, an inability to see logically or to simply "think" with higher cognitive and mental reasoning functions. They feel everything out, and this separates them from thinking. Also, there may be an overuse of the imaginative and intuitive, spiritual or psychic gifts due to Neptune; and a real lack of *grounding* with disregard to/detachment from physical reality. Practical duties and responsibilities may become neglected, essential material components will be overlooked, and fantasies and illusions become 'the norm.' This can lead to some of Pisces' worst traits, like extreme isolation and an unhealthy form of "lone wolf" syndrome. Community and family ties in addition to intimate and personal relationships suffer. Neptune transports this alchemical and transcendental Pisces to the depths of the astral and spiritual planes, so connections in the material and earthly plane disappear, or are weakened and suffer. It can be a form of addiction in itself for those Pisces who become "lost" in these places.

Other negative associations of this watery planet include hypersensitivity, being overly-emotional, and steering towards manipulation and self-deception. Actually, deception is intrinsically tied into too much Neptune influence. There is a heaviness associated with Neptune, one is prone to gaining weight or holding onto *emotional heaviness*- past painful memories or traumatic experiences. One may not be able to move forward with spiritual maturity, instead clinging onto distorted ways of thinking, behaving, acting and perceiving. "Getting stuck in the past" and allowing sensitives & insecurities to get the better of them, and spiritual naivety can dominate. Idiot compassion as well. Spiritual enlightenment and incredible creative and artistic-imaginative gifts are the other end of the spectrum, of course, however balance needs to be drawn. A strong Neptune influence for others such as air and fire signs can add an extra dimension of depth and spiritual insight, not to mention creative inspiration, into their lives. Yet, for Pisces, too much Neptune-focus and they will be lost in the deep blue sea, unable to find the beach.

Universal compassion, faith, purity and selflessness also come under Neptune's realm. Pisces sign can rise above the ego and individual to adopt a more selfless, collective, and holistically-encompassing viewpoint of reality. Poetry and seeing life with rose-colored or rainbow glasses can be deeply positive…. Neptune allows Pisces to speak from the soul and display almost non-human forms of boundless compassion. There is an angelic link with this planet. Interestingly enough, the glyph (astrological symbol) for Neptune is the trident, symbolic of Poseidon (God of the Seas). This is a crescent on top of a cross which portrays matter and spirit, the crescent represents receptivity and the journey towards spiritual enlightenment and illumination. The placement of it on top of the cross signifies a deep yearning to break free for material bonds and chains. One desires to rise above the mundane and physical world or achieve transcendental states of consciousness. Material structures and limitations are strongly rejected by many Pisces, and in the positive way this manifests as Buddhahood, Christ consciousness, or embodying a spiritual and purified mind, body & spirit. Purification.

 *Neptune's glyph*

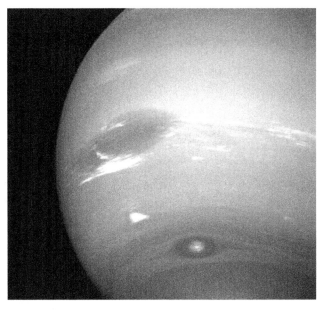

### *Further evaluation of Neptune's glyph (Pisces' ruling planetary symbol)*

We can learn a lot from Neptune's glyph. The three arrows can be seen as representing the sky and heavens. They point upwards showing a desire to break free from the bonds of the material planes below. Transcendental union, in other words. connecting and aligning with the soul and spiritual dimensions. Three is a very significant number in both numerology, the ancient study of numbers and the qualities they bring, and astrology, too. 3 symbolizes the *holy trinity*, a unification of mind, body & spirit. Number 3 also represents past, present, and future and this integral to a developed and evolved Pisces' philosophy. Pisces recognizes the timeless and nonlinear nature of reality, but they also frequently visit the past and future for insight and self-discovery. To a Pisces, past, present and future are interlinked. Oneness is a concept and reality they've mastered, Neptune provides the understanding that we are not defined by our past and that we can learn from our pains, wounds and memories, further learning how to become conscious and aware in the present moment. Ancestral and karmic wounds can be transcended. And, being conscious of ways to tune into the future, such as through lucid and shamanic dreaming, strengthening psychic gifts, and staying committed to one's "future self," is integral to a Pisces' path. Connecting to our spiritual selves whilst remaining grounded, rooted in the physical body and the earthly realm, is the ultimate interpretation of '3.' Finally, great visionary works have been created under Neptune's influence. This massive water planet is 'forward thinking,' idealistic, success and achievement oriented (in the creative and imaginative worlds), and gifted.

✧ ◆ ✧

*Neptune's Motto & Mantra*:

"I would be comfortable giving up all worldly possessions and living in an ashram or monastery. I could meditate every day and connect with Source and Spirit, free from materialistic desires and the greed and needs of the physical world. I am happy to live a life of servitude and selfless charity, or simply be one with nature, surrendering to divine simplicity... A peaceful and simple life is for me, and if I have to dedicate my life to something beyond myself, I could.

Yet, I would also thrive in a path that leads to my success and financial prosperity. Abundance is my birthright, I am meant to shine! I would be overjoyed to use my creative and artistic gifts to uplift the collective vibration of humanity, further contributing to healing on a global & planetary level. As for being my own boss? *I Am a boss*. I'm free to shine in self-employment and attract wealth and new connections on my path. I'm not afraid of accomplishment or big achievements, so chasing fame or wealth can be integral to my spiritual journey.

So long as I am true to myself, live with divine grace and integrity, and channel my energy into spiritual, empathic, creative and imaginative ways of seeing and being; I am free and content. Life is a dream and I am the captain, the passenger and the ship."

## Dream Signs: Healing, Insightful & Positive

As a Pisces with my Venus also in Pisces, and Moon in Cancer (another watery, psychically in tune, and subconsciously and instinctively enhanced sign), I feel intuitively that many Pisces will have had similar dreams to me. At least the overall sign or symbol will be shared and resonate. This section is more aligned with a dream interpretation-style approach, whereas other ones are focused on the underlying and main themes of dreaming for a Pisces. (Actual dream themes are explored in depth later.)

### Alien Spaceships

Spaceships and alien crafts seem to make their way into this sign's dreams, and frequently. During celestial and key world events mystical Pisces has a lot of dreams about spaceships and aliens visiting them. By 'celestial' I am referring to Lunar and Solar Eclipses, key timeline moments such as the 2012 Grand Cycle shift, and significant Equinoxes and Solstices. Alien beings of light or clearly from a different world and dimension "visit" to show some core part of yourself. Depending on what chapter you're in and how/where you're currently operating, they will either show what you need to balance and integrate, embody and embrace- shadow elements and personality traits; or, where you're going and what you're doing right. Key insights into your path, soul or spirit alignment and purpose, and future self. Aliens are representations of our soul and psyche. They have mastered the laws of the universe and can therefore travel through it in advanced craft. Aliens are mirrors of *higher consciousness*. So, mystical and spiritually evolved Pisces will often dream of alien visitations, contact or spacecraft flying down into the earth. Overall, this symbolizes a merging of heaven and earth, divine and spiritual consciousness being birthed or manifested into the physical realm, and higher self and lower/human/primal self uniting.

## Animals

Butterflies, dolphins and other healing types of 'spirit animals' make their way into a Pisces' dreamscape. Mystical and mythological creatures like unicorns, fairies, and dragons as well. All the Zodiac signs can be shown as spirit animals or receive messages and subconscious insights from a number of spirit animals, but there is a common theme among Pisces. Being feminine in nature and deeply sensitive, soulful, and peace-loving, there are few that are worthy of a mention.

### Butterflies

A butterfly symbolizes transformation and awakening of the Soul. This spirit animal often shows itself to Pisces in dreams frequently throughout childhood and early adolescence to teenage years. Also, at any point later in life during a particularly significant life chapter and transition. Butterfly is a symbol for the breakthrough, breaking free of limitations and restrictions, and embracing freedom. Leaving the past in the past and stepping into a new chapter and cycle, which is always rooted in self-evolution and a Higher Self version of oneself. Butterflies also symbolize soul gifts, creative talents, unique artistry and the imagination, and further spiritual insight and intuition. This spirit animal shows how Pisces can accept change with grace and eloquence, whilst stepping into self-alignment and beauty, abundance, dreams, psyche and shadow self integration, and personal inspiration.

### Dolphins

Dolphins are very close to a Pisces' heart. Dolphins are symbolic of harmony, balance, and feeling comfortable in the emotional and instinctive realms. Dolphins are intelligent, perceptive and wise and can further communicate telepathically. This all represents Pisces' true nature. They possess advanced powers of communication (telepathy) and incredible instincts. But, they're also playful and big lovers of family and community. This is something Pisces can learn. Pisces is usually a lone wolf, at least in their teens and 20's. It can take a long time for a young Pisces on a journey of self-discovery to "find themselves," and embrace maturer cycles with a focus on relationships and dropping boundaries (once healed, and whole and mature within). They want to be the independent lone wolf and free-spirit forever. Or, it at least appears this way. Yet, Pisces needs relationships and intimacy- they desire love and companionship on the deepest of levels. This is the 'inner pull' as seen in their glyph/symbol, the two fish swimming in opposite directions. In terms of the dolphin, Pisces can learn to balance their need for independence with community, friendship &

social ties. Being a lone wolf or swimming off solo may work in early life, but by their mid to late twenties all Pisces come to realize that it is human nature to want a family, and/or to integrate in communities with strong social foundations and an emphasis on connection.

Other meanings include being peaceful in any situation or circumstance, gentleness, and possessing inner strength with a calm mental and psychological disposition. Playfulness and joy can be embraced- 'lightening up' and being more care-free too. And, cooperation, compromise and adaptability! Dolphins equally represent the ability to speak one's truth, thus opening up being clear and transparent in emotions and feelings. There's a sense of fearlessness, bravery and courage associated with the dolphin. Selflessness is a trait shared by dolphins and Pisces, and Pisces are very much like a dolphin in many ways. Multidimensional wisdom is available when a dolphin appears in dreams, thus there is always an accompanying sense of liberation and absolute freedom. A dolphin is a very positive sign to see in a dream; Pisces, pay attention to the close bonds in your life, as these hold the answers to your happiness.

*Swans*

Inner beauty, femininity, and eloquence are some of the main messages of the swan. This spirit animal resonates more with female Pisces but it's still relevant to men. The swan is a graceful and eloquent creature with strong instincts. If a swan appears, it's asking you to strengthen your intuition and listen to your soul, psyche and innermost self. What are your needs at this time? Are you currently with a soulmate or lover, and how do you feel about this? Swans symbolize companionship and soul deep love. Swans are a reflection of the subconscious mind, portraying our feelings towards love, intimacy, and companionship. There's a strong feminine and nurturing energy here to be learned. Spiritual evolution, maturity, faith and hope, awakening to your soul and spiritual gifts, divination, tranquility, loyalty and devotion can all be understood.

Swans also teach free spirited and wanderlusty Pisces the meaning of commitment and monogamy, if they're open to it. Swans mate for life. Once they begin courtship and have entered into companionship there's not much that will break them apart. The bond is deep and eternal, and they're not like other birds who mate for one season or a few. The polyamory or adultery seen in many animal species is not shared with swans. They're a key message here. Purity, partnership, balance and harmony are all lessons of the swan. This animal usually appears to offer insight when romance is on their mind.

*Birds*

Birds are frequently seen by Pisces on a multidimensional plane, or in an otherworldly way. The astral and ethereal senses are heightened, therefore Pisces could quite literally experience a dream with birds in nature where there is an energetic shield, sparkly or celestial blur, or divine and spiritual energy permeating the scene. I myself have had many dreams like this. Birds represent freedom and liberation from material or physical structures. Limits and restrictions can be transcended. Personally, I've witnessed myself as an observer and as pure spirit/ether watching myself float freely up, existing on the subtle planes and realms like birds do. Their energy and spirit uplifted me so I was able to fly like them. The feeling and inner knowing? *There are multiple realms and dimensions of being.* Evolving consciousness to a higher dimension, and a spiritual vibration, allows us to transcend the earthly realm and proceed to higher heights. Shifts occur when we work towards a light body, i.e. embodying more light, and thus moving away from a carbon body (through dense and heavy, unhealthy foods) and heavy emotions, toxic realities, and lower perspectives. One is able to see things from a higher perspective with wisdom relating to the astral realms and spiritual maturity. One specific dream I remember very vividly (and is currently written in my Dream Journal), involved a *blackbird*. I've actually had a few symbolic dreams with blackbirds…

In this one, I was in a magical (ethereal) garden, very "spacey" with an otherworldly feel. A blackbird was flying higher and higher while I was rising with the bird. We were staring into each other's eyes, it was an intense and mystical form of eye-gazing! The more secure the bond and connection was (through eye contact) the higher I rose. The moment I lost eye contact the cord and bridge broke, and I dropped to the ground. The instinctual knowing from the dream and subsequent dream message was that birds and animals can transport us to magical lands. They help to raise our vibrations through the ethereal and mystical-spiritual energy and wisdom they bring. When looking at their actual spiritual symbolism and energetic meaning we see the truth in this instinctive knowing. Blackbirds signify seeing beyond the veil of illusion and mastering mysteries of the universe... This bird links to shamanic healing and wisdom, a deep connection to both nature and spirit; and accessing unlimited potential and personal power. Positive alchemy, magic and transformation can come about with blackbirds appearing on the astral planes in dreams. The second meaning of my dream was interesting, as I was shown an "astral vision" of my old circle of friends (who were still operating in a very low and toxic energy- a lot of drugs, substances, alcohol/poison and addictions). I was meant to leave them, as projected and portrayed in 'floating higher' with the bird- being transported to a magical and *higher dimensional* world and reality…


*Unicorns*

Unicorns are mythological creatures. The message of the unicorn is to step into purity, innocence and your inner magic. Unicorns symbolize child-like innocence, the inner child, and liberated joy free from fear of judgment or false perception. They are purity in essence, and hold a strong spiritual vibration. Dreams and wishes can be realized and achieved when a unicorn comes into a Pisces' dreams. It's all about stepping into power and self-alignment, further embodying self-love while reclaiming your innocence. Purity births power and connection, intuition and instincts. This is a wonderful dream omen and message for Pisces, it shows them they are on the right path and should continue to access soul and spiritual gifts. Psychic ability, clairvoyance and the other clairs- clairaudience and clairsentience, and telepathic communication can also be accessed. Faith, hope, universal compassion and unconditional love can equally be realized and embodied.

*Dragons*

Although typically associated with the fire signs, dragons are another mythological creature finding its way into the Pisces dreamspace. Dragons are all about purpose, power and destiny. Soul talents, soul path and purpose, and soul alignment can all be understood with the presence of a dragon. They represent your soul's fire, the burning desires within waiting to be birthed into the world. This is really empowering for a Pisces who is usually quite receptive and passive, watery and sensitive. A dragon can show Pisces that spirit, the universe, or whatever higher power they believe in (or simply the subconscious itself) has their back. They are supported and have invisible but benevolent support and divine guidance. The dragon is essentially about soul resonance, and stepping into personal power and leadership so other like-minded souls and kindred spirits can vibe from you. Or learn from you if you're called to a higher calling, like becoming a teacher, wayshower, or visionary. Other main associations which you can connect to and live up to include success, achievements & accomplishments, wisdom, self-protection, universal protection, confidence, fearlessness, and an immensely passionate and self-expressive nature and personality.

**Beautiful Nature and Landscapes**

The Pisces Spirit is defined by a love of an affinity with nature. Planet earth is seen as a living entity to Pisces, for they recognize consciousness flows through all living things. An integral belief of Pisces is the concept of "oneness," interconnectedness. Oneness flows through all living things from humans to animals, plant life and the planet itself. Gaia is the spirit of our planet, and Pisces sees the non-physical, energetic and spiritual/ethereal energy of our planet. Because of such a powerful and close bond, they will regularly dream of being in beautiful landscapes and natural environments. A lot can be learned from a simple dream symbol. One's emotions and feelings surrounding the nature spot signifies the message and purpose of the dream, however the theme is always the same; any sort of contentedness and peace signifies Pisces being in tune with their soul gifts. Their true self is free to shine when they dream of nature. Of course, feeling disoriented, out of place, or emotionally pained, chaotic, or imbalanced portrays a different aspect of the dream message- how healing is needed. It's always important for Pisces to look at the feeling and message, symbolism and guidance surrounding the dream context.

*Caves*

A cave is another common dream symbol guiding a naive Pisces back to wholeness and healing. Caves are symbolic of darkness, however with darkness comes light. Pisces dreams of caves with a light somewhere, either inside as a source of power and protection, light and self-awareness, or around or outside the cave. Coming back home to their true selves is the main message of this positive dream message. Returning to source, to their spiritual selves and authenticity, and to self-alignment indicates a Pisces needs to work on their boundaries or their shadow self. Pisces will dream of a cave when they have become lost in darkness, addiction, self-destructive behavior, denial or loss and separation. Anything can trigger a sensitive fish, so rejection or abandonment or other core themes as outlined in *Pisces Shadow* will result in caves and other "dark" spaces. These dreams are not dark to Pisces. They recognize the light and the asking of spirit and their subconscious to return to their true nature. Celestial light emanates from within the cave, or there is a spark and healing energy surrounding the inner or outer layers of the cave. Cave symbols are gateways to Pisces, they're not dark places and there is always a greater lesson or truth to be experienced.

## Celestial Light Beings or Angels

The same as what has been shared for Alien Spaceships is true for light beings and angels, ascended masters and beings existing on the higher planes. Celestial transits and cosmic activity tends to highlight these experiences for Pisces. But a Pisces can and will dream about these evolved beings at any time, in any place. The Pisces mind is attuned to a higher dimension- even when they don't know it (consciously). Angelic life forms and actual or metaphorical ascended masters present themselves to pass on wisdom, guidance or some key message. They emit a glow and sparkle. Divine light and warmth, openness and a strong heart center energy is always common. The third eye and higher self too. Pisces will instinctively know that the 'dream character' with which they are speaking exists above and beyond this realm, so there is a link to the divine and light realms present. *The purpose?* These dream symbols always work in Pisces' best interests and are here to lovingly and benevolently guide them, back to their hearts and higher selves.

## Floating away from the past

Past cycles, relationships and friendships that have out-served their purpose are common. Pisces has visions or ethereal (other-worldly) dreams where they, literally, float away from friends, old lovers, or outdated cycles and chapters in their life. Pisces sees in a type of x-ray vision that makes them *know* their higher self is steering them away from past cycles and relationships. There is usually a feeling of hope and optimism, although there may be some temporary sadness and despair. Pisces has a unique sense of mission. The path of a Pisces can be rare, as they tend to 'leave it all behind'- transcend individual needs and their old timeline and history- for something aligned with selfless service, soulful purpose, or extraordinary projects and paths. Inspiring vision and groundbreaking creativity is the Pisces sign. Old friendship circles and cycles that were/are part of their past come through as subconscious reminders or insights in the dream worlds. They may observe themselves as onlookers to the dream, thus completely at one with their subconscious (subconsciousness). Or they could be perceiving from a first person viewpoint, or a mixture. Many Pisces can *transcend* the 3-dimensional limitations of the material world, i.e. they merge with the collective sub/consciousness. A young and sensitive, often dreamy and spaced out, Pisces must leave behind the immaturity and naivety of their younger selves, which includes old friendships and relationships that have served their purpose, and evolve to new heights. Personal growth and self-evolution is always available to this sign.


**A Fountain**

Many Pisces dream of a fountain as the centerpiece of some unique and specific event, dream scenario or scene. The fountain sits as the symbol for which the dreamer knows there is a message, a lesson to be learned and understood. Characters, conversation and events then play out around the fountain. The fountain is, of course, symbolic of water; emotions, feelings, subtle impressions and subconscious reflections. Whatever is occuring in the dream provides a clue as to what the presence of the fountain is trying to convey. *How did you feel in the dream, in relation to the overall message? What specific words or phrases can you remember? Who were the dream characters- how did they dress, what were their archetypes/personas, and what wisdom did they bring?* The fountain is the symbol. The events surrounding the fountain are the subconscious message. The key with these dreams involving a fountain is to pay attention to the characters and interactions, everything making up the sustenance of the dream scenario or message. As long as there is a fountain, one can be sure that there is some deeper insight wanting to be shown regarding one's emotional and personal life.


**"Other Key Symbols"**

Golden temples, Diamonds, Christ-like figures, crystalline structures, temples, and magical books with ancient and timeless stories to tell are core key symbols of Pisces. Pisces is able to access other worlds. They're connected to portals of cosmic, higher, divine and spiritual/mystical consciousness… The array of symbols available here is limitless. Anything considered sublime and mystical, or godly and heavenly, comes under Pisces' dreaming abilities. We look at these symbols more in *'Recurring Dreams.'*

## Subconscious Reminders

The subconscious mind works in harmony with Pisces, it doesn't work against them nor is there a block or discord. You may have noticed that we haven't mentioned any other signs here, there's been very little comparisons or references to differences. The focus has been solely on Pisces. Well, there's one thing you should know to help you understand this sign better. Each star/Zodiac sign has its own set of unique traits and characteristics. Astrology is very real and equally as fascinating. Pisces and the other two water signs, Cancer and Scorpio, are *watery, emotional, intuitive, psychic/clairvoyant, imaginatively gifted, instinctive and spiritually advanced* (open, evolved, aware). But the same can't be said about all the signs of the Zodiac! Yes, each is unique, yet *Pisces* is one of 3 so deeply connected to instinctive and subconscious forces. For example, the fire signs Aries, Leo and Sagittarius get their energy and subsequent gifts from the Sun, and fiery planets like Mars and Jupiter. They are masculine (while Pisces is feminine). They are yang (while Pisces is yin). And they excel in areas completely opposite, apparently, to Pisces. So, when it is said that the subconscious mind works in harmony with them and further not against them, this shouldn't be undervalued.


### Water element associations...

Because water is symbolic of emotions and the subconscious in general, those born into the Pisces sign will experience dreams in a unique way. Healing, insightful and positive dream signs will almost *always* be linked to the dreamer's (Pisces') emotions and internal world. This is the realm of feelings and subtle impressions, beliefs and the like! Essentially, this means Pisces will draw a message or piece of wisdom relating to *relationships*, *intimate connections*, and their *emotional bonds* virtually 99.9+% of the time. Anything relating to the relationships in their life, in waking life, will be given pointers and clues in their dreams. Secondly, Pisces is prone to *prophetic dreams*- the ability to see or envision the future, or aspects of it. This is again linked to the water element.

## Dream Signs: Mindful Warnings

There are certain archetypes and dreams that occur for Pisces which are not so positive. These can be seen as bad, or harmful and verging on the 'nightmare' category. Red flags, danger signals, messages and lessons- situations in waking life that may pose a risk or have 'destruction' status. Dream signs in this category are the messages from the subconscious mind aimed to help a lost or ungrounded fish. It's easy for sensitive Pisces to become lost in the infinite seas and waters in which they swim, so their subconscious selves often send them dream signals to realign them on course. One of the beautiful things about Pisces is, however, that they don't feel fear in the same way others do. People have many fears, it's natural. Pisces' fear is the fear of fear itself. Thus, they recognize- and quite clearly- how the *darkness* 'aka' the shadow realms and dark, murky and intimidating depths of the dreamspace, are a source of *creation* and *potential.* Whereas other humans might be generally terrified or wake up shivering or screaming, a Pisces will feel a sort of indifference, an apathy and sympathy. The best analogy to use here is to imagine an animal who feels comfort in the dark. Owls are nocturnal… They are able to see and be at peace in the depths of the night, when the moon's magic is out to work & play. This is Pisces sign.

Expanding on, this signifies that Pisces will take the darkness and disturbing depths of the mystical dreamworlds and find the teaching or message in them. Pisces is gifted with the gifts of foresight, prophecy, clairvoyance, finding comfort in the dark, divine feminine wisdom, and spiritual insight. Guess what? *These are the energetic associations and symbolisms of Owls as well!* (You'll see the symbolic link here in 'Shamanic dreaming.')

Let's now explore some of the main warning signs and dark dream symbols of Pisces.

**Evil Fairytale Characters (+ Mythological Creatures)**

You may have heard of the expression "fairy-tale love"...? Well, this is associated with Pisces! Pisces are pure romantics and complete believers in fairytale love. With this comes its shadow, the opposite of the light and wonderful creatures found in fairy tales and magical stories. Pisces are extremely connected to fantasy, mystic lands and dreamworlds, and ethereal-spiritual layers of reality. Their imagination is advanced beyond comprehension (to a non-Pisces). Being so "at one" with it all, with the lightness, the darkness, and the openness to self-mastery and spiritual growth; means they inevitably have quite a lot of dark dreams. Some of their deepest fears can come through in the forms of mythical and evil fairytale-like characters. To a Pisces, it's real. Just as the 'light' dreams are real, the 'dark' ones are real too. Once they're there in the dreamspace it's as real as the air that surrounds them. This can ruin a sensitive and naive Pisces' dream and waking life experience, leading them to escapist tendencies and depression, which are usually unconscious. Evil witches, poltergeists, dark shadows and predatory beasts all represent some dark force or emotion trying to take over their life. It is rare for Pisces to have dreams of dark aliens, and Pisces knows on some instinctive level that 'aliens' symbolize higher consciousness. Virtually all Pisces recognize that aliens or other life forms in the universe exist on a frequency of light and benevolence.

But, mythological animals and characters will still sometimes make their way into dreams. Evil witches represent the evil feminine, the dark side of Mother Earth and feminine energy. Pisces is a feminine sign, of course- they are receptive and passive, introverted and more repressed than masculine signs. They have a deep connection to the earth and the planet, therefore dreaming of an 'evil witch' shows they are out of balance with themselves. There's an internal distortion or block, or potentially faulty perception and belief or mindset. Witches are empathic, intuitive, powerful and benevolent beings, they're medicine women and healers, shamanically inclined and connected to the cosmic life force and Spirit of the universe. They're not evil! So dreaming of a scary and evil witch is the inner Mother, Lover, Nurturer and Sister trying to come out. All in all, it represents a disconnection from Spirit and the divine feminine. Predatory beasts symbolize a disconnect from one's primal and instinctive self, relating to animal instincts. Lust, sexuality, and needs for intimacy and physical connection are associated with predatory beasts. Assuming you are running away from one and frightened the message is that one is running away from their primal self. The inner shadow too. One thing Pisces needs to learn (what with being so spiritual) is that they have a physical body. As for poltergeists, evil characters, and dark shadows, there is a need for shadow self integration. These dream signs suggest the Pisces is out of balance. They need to integrate a repressed or denied part of themselves, otherwise they will fall into depression, despair, self-denial, or escapism, or the like.

## Entrapment

Having such an expansive character means Pisces sign loves to feel free. They often dream of oceans, open spaces, and unseen mystical worlds. They have a lot of dreams of the ocean and water in general, and in these spaces they feel at home. They're full of comfort and ease. But, being a dual sign they sometimes have much darker dreams. It is common for this water sign to be stuck, trapped, or seriously hurt through confinement. Expansiveness is met with entrapment and limitation, forced enclosures and suppressions leading to real danger and threat of life (in the dream space). A loss of self is one of the greatest fears of a Pisces. They fear spiritual disconnection, misalignment, and a separation from Source more than anything itself. The other side of this they need to feel connected- a Pisces thrives in interconnectedness and oneness. Not only do they thrive in feelings of oneness and unity but they also require it for their survival. Unlike other signs, survival to Pisces is psychological, emotional and spiritual, if there is no telepathic (mental), empathic (emotional) or harmonious & loving (spiritual) connection, they become lost, down and depressed. Further, they go into darkness and despair, or can do. Connection is everything to them.

Darkness is the root of all fear and heartache, yet darkness represents fear to Pisces. It's also their source of enlightenment and inspiration, they learn their greatest lessons from the darkness and shadow realms. This may sound confusing or hard to understand, but it makes sense to them; it's reality, in fact. Light comes out of darkness and the dark is both something to be feared (because it entraps them and keeps them stuck in a state of separation) and a pathway to healing & growth simultaneously. Pisces sign is naturally more comfortable with their shadow selves than any other sign. Faith, purity, hope, soul alignment, and understanding the great mysteries of the universe are some of Pisces' greatest gifts. So, going back to entrapping worlds and dream scenarios, it can be a very scary place which affects their psyche and soul on a deep level. A Pisces may subconsciously or unconsciously give themselves *tests*. On their pursuit of spiritual evolution and self-mastery- integral ingredients to a Pisces' path- they push themselves through trials & tribulations. In waking life, they set their intentions for self-development and spiritual mastery, so when it comes to dreaming their subconscious honors their request. Their subconscious mind works closely with their conscious mind.

## Sleep Paralysis… the Terrifying type

The last sub-topic links to sleep paralysis too. One of the most intense things any star sign can go through is sleep paralysis. This is the inability to wake up, the mind is 'stuck' between dimensions, between the dream world and waking life. Your mind knows you're awake, as on some level you are awake, but a part of you is still sleeping or dreaming. The result is a severe form of compression where your body feels completely trapped and weighed down. Dark and fearful thoughts can arise and sometimes these are accompanied by mystical or ethereal visions, or the like. Profound and vivid imagery linked to a dream previously having. Quite simply, you can't wake yourself up or find the link and connection to your physical body, even though you're fully aware that you're awake. Your body becomes trapped and anchored to the bed or ground. The mind can conjure up the worst thoughts and images in this state of disassociation. Depending which way round the sleep paralysis occurs, i.e. are you trying to avoid sleep in a state of exhaustion; has the sleep paralysis kicked in before you've had a chance to fall into a deep and relaxed sleep, so you attempt to prevent yourself from sleeping to avoid the undeniable dread of paralysis? Or can you not wake up after a period of deep sleep due to the paralysis being so intense? If the former, it is a twisted game! You know you desperately need sleep but won't succumb to the dark spiral. If the latter, the same is true, but you still *can't* wake up.

Sleep paralysis is particularly intense for spiritual, sensitive and emotional Pisces. They're naturally attuned to the subtle worlds, meaning that they feel things more intently. I myself have experienced some extraordinarily bad periods of sleep paralysis. In one of them, I actually woke myself up while still asleep, to tell myself that I needed to wake myself up! Being so *psychic*, *clairvoyant*, and *multidimensionally activated* I was able to "pre-warn" myself, in my dream/sleep space, to inform me that I was about to experience the most intense sleep paralysis I had and ever would experience. Luckily, I had a friend sleeping over (this was in my late-ish teenage years) who was there to offer his care and love. In fact, I woke myself up screaming utterly terrified. I've experienced a lot of otherworldly, dark and lucid dreams, but I can inform you that was the only time I was ever truly frightened of an experience that occurred on the astral planes (during sleep and the dream-waking life crossover). It was intense.

The point of sharing this personal story is to, hopefully, convey just how powerful sleep paralysis can be for a Pisces and how bad it can get. Vivid, graphic, deep, intense, lifelike and wholly realistic to the point of being mistaken for non-fantasy, sleep paralysis represents Pisces' worst nightmare; fear of fear itself. It is like being trapped in an eternal and never-ending spiral that drags them down to the darkest places known to mankind. The most interesting part is that they have this experience to simply experience. It's like a part of their subconscious or the universe itself says, *'You've asked for the deepest and most advanced type of dream experiences possible… here you are!'* I can confirm that there isn't really any "point" to such extreme paralysis- there's no emotional insight, relationship advice, subconscious wisdom, healing power (direct) or anything linked to any theme Pisces can access for learning. It simply happens because it can, to show this mystic creature the depths and infinite possibilities of the universe. It is an experience Pisces can add to their list to confirm their knowledge that the universe and cosmos itself is limitless, expansive and full of mystery. One thing I would say it provides, however, is the effects it can have upon waking. How does emotional and sometimes super-sensitive Pisces deal with this experience? Do they fall into fear and self-denial, repression and isolation or addiction? Or do they step into their power and into the light? Questions every Pisces asks with such an intense experience.

## Loss, Rejection, and Fear

The fear of rejection is one of the most- if not the most- basic instinctive fear and drive of the Pisces star sign. Fear and love- unity- are tied into each other. Our fears lead to our desires and motivations in life, so being scared on a soul level of rejection and loss creates Pisces to strive for *connection*. The desire for intimacy and emotional connection drives every single thing a Pisces does in life, whether it be positive and connected to their light and strengths or negative and acting from shadow or wounds. A loss of connection is a loss of self, in Pisces' eye... They crave soul bonding or at least deep psychological, emotional and spiritual bonds. This is enhanced even more if they've experienced lots of rejection and abandonment in early life. The other way to look at it, is that these experiences were created by their psyche or soul to help them grow. It is often the bad or hard experiences in life that make us stronger, and provide for our greatest strengths. So, Pisces' fear of loss, including actual rejection and/or abandonment, sets them up for incredible talents and inner strength to draw from later in life. In dreams, this will manifest as experiencing the pain and heartache of loss. Pisces can feel emotions in the dreamspace just as powerful as they do in waking life, sometimes more intense. Dreaming of being rejected by a mother or father, or abandoned by a lover or soulmate are common. This is true specifically in teenage and young adult life. If wounds haven't been healed, an adult Pisces may see dream scenarios of a child or baby being taken away from them, or quite literally sobbing connected to the vibration of soul loss & heartbreak over some separation (friendship, family bond, love bond, child, etc.).

## Bad Omens of Nature

Some of the most common bad omens of nature include hurricanes, storms, and overpowering or violent waves. These symbolize a passionate relationship or relationships with much energy and vitality, yet equal measures of growth and struggle. This may be a soulmate relationship currently in or about to enter, and the general message is that there is likely to be some toxic (and karmic) love elements to work through. There will be many joyous moments but it will ultimately be full of lessons, trials and tribulations to make one stronger. Stormy or rocky times are also ahead. Emotions will be stirred, and Pisces is most likely about to see some intense life events manifest. They may be going through a breakup, turmoil or upheaval; it would appear as if this is a time of transition and tricky growth, however there is light at the end of the tunnel, and the storm will eventually pass. This 'negative' or 'dark' dream omen for Pisces is a clue to embrace the current rough times ahead because there is significant illumination and positive transformation within it. Nature is within us all and Pisces knows this better than many others. Hurricanes, storms and violent or aggressive seas and bodies of water show this sensitive sign that they need to keep their emotions in check, and that something in their life is currently out of balance. There is distortion and possible hardship ahead.

## Blood and Meat

Finally, Being a water sign signifies empathy, sensitivity, and compassion. Blood and meat are generally considered bad signs, therefore. Blood can represent the shadow self and key lessons not being integrated, or some disharmony with oneself. Blood is symbolic of distortion and inner disunity. Meat is also a bad sign. Being watery and empathic, Pisces is often prone towards vegetarianism or veganism. They're certainly the most compassionate beings out of the bunch. Meat is essentially a dead animal thus there could be some signs of death and destruction associated here. If meat or blood appears in your dream it could very well be your subconscious telling you you're out of alignment, not in tune with your soul or true self. The secondary meaning is deception. Society informs us we 'need' meat to survive or for protein, but this isn't the case. Meat appearing in a dream suggests that someone may be deceiving or manipulating you or that they don't have your best interests at heart. Alternatively it could represent a fire or air sign, two elemental signs that aren't too compatible with you. They may be neglecting or overlooking your emotional needs or simply don't care as much as you believe. As a water sign, Pisces is compassionate and deeply empathic but this doesn't mean everyone else is. Water is attuned to a different frequency, and while blood and meat may represent passion and primal or animalistic desires respectively- to the air and fire signs- to empathic emotional creatures they have entirely different dream meanings. Pisces needs to pay attention to the friendships and acquaintances in their life with these two dream omens. It's useful to spend some time in meditation and introspection to suss out the true colors and intentions of the people in your life.

## Dream Symbols

Firstly, **water** is the main dream symbol of this sensitive sign. Most to all of the other dream symbols for Pisces originate from water, with a few exceptions. Water symbolizes the subconscious itself, the deep and infinite waters of creation. Water is creation, actually; the vastness and eternal nature of life and self. But, water extends beyond creation and infinity itself, it also represents emotions, internal feelings, and subtle impressions. Dreaming of any bodies of water like oceans, lakes, the sea, waterfalls, rain, ponds, and rivers shows some aspect of one's emotions and the subconscious. Holistically, water defines one's inner world and all the impressions and feelings that accompany. The context and environment shows further insight into what the dream symbol is showing, i.e. the message.

Water represents emotions, moods and inner feelings, essentially. There is a reason why virtually every human on earth feels a sense of peace and belonging when visiting a beach and ocean or seaside, and this is most true for Pisces. The great and beautiful vastness of the ocean's waves provides a deep and ancestral feeling of belonging, comfort, security, and surrender... one feels "at home" and as if they're connected to the planet in an unexplainable, ethereal and otherworldly way. This is due to the sea's link to the subconscious. Water is holistically seen to symbolize the subconscious mind. It also has ties to the unknown, the 'infinite waters of creation,' and Source energy. A healthy embodiment of water has a number of benefits and positive results and this is the Pisces sign's main dream symbol. Further water is receptive, passive, "flowy" (relating to going with the flow/surrendering), adaptable and yin in nature. Yin is of course magnetic, feminine and dark- the inner and outer darkness with close ties to the shadow self. Water can be seen as the opposite of fire, as yin (water) is the opposite and counterpart to yang (fire). Understanding this can help you understand the themes of a Pisces' dream world.

So, this dream symbol signifies Pisces is *able to express their feelings and inner moods effortlessly and eloquently*. Emotions aren't chaotic, disruptive or irrational, nor are they screamed or shouted at others in a destructive way like when there is too much water or too little, the latter resulting in frustration building up and leading to sporadic outbursts! Or manipulation, projection, etc. One doesn't project unhealed or imbalanced emotions on others, and is generally quite eloquent and kind in their personal expressions. There are constant and harmonious (healthy) emotional releases. Water relates to **memory** too, so when there is sufficient water one is able to remember situations and past experiences in a useful and helpful way. The subconscious mind represents emotions, moods, inner currents, and instinctual and intuitive desires, as you're aware, yet it also represents **vision.** Psychic and spiritual gifts and abilities come under water's influence, those with strong water in their charts tend to be empathic, intuitive, clairvoyant and psychic, or spiritually gifted in some way. They can tune into universal archetypes and ideas and sense things others miss. Thus, Pisces is the embodiment of these innate gifts and powers. Intuition is activated and expanded and advanced forms of psychic perception & intuitive/instinctual powers are amplified. Having a healthy flow of the water element in one's life is essential for Pisces and is further shown in the dreamworlds through positive feelings and symbols.

Pisces uses water as a sort of "magical compass." In addition to the things just mentioned, this sign also astral projects, lucid dreams, and receives guidance and profound imagery, symbolism and wisdom during dreamtime. One's *Higher Self* becomes active during dreams, the higher self relating to the 'higher mind.' There is no better way to understand the world of a Pisces than to explore the meanings & energetic associations of water and the Higher Self. Pisces tend to have a very active and open *Third Eye chakra...* Pisces are mostly introverted or introspective. Society is predominantly masculine and extroverted, there is a large emphasis and focus on fire, ambition, solar energy, competition and aspects & qualities relating to the masculine. What about the Moon and the feminine? This is why Pisces thrives in dream time. They draw their power and awareness from the inner worlds and layers of reality which the water element and symbol helps with. In society, "watery qualities" tend to be seen as something strange, weird, or peculiar, or at the very least something 'different.' But there is nothing odd about water and emotional, sensitive traits that accompany it. If anything, a Pisces would say being disconnected from psychic and subtle energy and the emotional-spiritual realms is weird! Twisted distortion. The world is largely focused on 'outer to inner' while Pisces is connected with 'inner to outer.'

Do you think it's strange how children who are deeply imaginative and artistic at school are labeled as 'different,' 'introverts,' or 'unique?' A young Pisces' dreams are full of imagery and vivid symbolism. There is an intuitive and sensual knowing even in their youth. A young Pisces may not feel comfortable sharing their dreams- trust is developed later in life, when they know there are people who see and understand them, however, Pisces have amazing dreams all the same. Their imagination is free to come to life, Neptune shine's its big and dreamy astral rays on this little fish. Society may tell us certain things are "wrong" or "weird" but this doesn't stop a Pisces from being themselves. Perceiving dream symbolism as avenues for learning and self-discovery are *integral* to a Pisces' life and self. And this lets them align with imagery and profound visions many others can't. Remember the key words (personality traits): *imagination, vision, intuition and spirituality*. Mystical and psychic too.

## Mermaids

It is very common for Pisces to dream of mermaids, especially females. Mermaids represent a deep affinity with the sea and with the emotional realm. There are multiple meanings and dream messages of the mermaid, but the primary one is feeling comfortable in the depths of the subconscious and spiritual realms. There is an otherworldly feeling of the mermaids, of being from another time and space. Shapeshifting is associated with mermaids. Mermaids are of both land and sea, they can navigate energies of the earth and humankind and water and the oceans simultaneously. "Breathing underwater" is symbolic of feeling content with life's currents and the many feelings, impressions, emotions, and experiences life brings. They're here to show you, as a Pisces, the multidimensional nature of time, space, and reality- how there are multiple frequencies and dimensions existing. Mermaids link to Atlantis. Atlantis is a higher dimensional consciousness of earth, a time where humans lived in harmony with nature. They were connected to their source of spiritual power, higher truth and wisdom, universal awareness, intuition, and advanced instinctual and psychic gifts. Many believe Atlantis is only a dimension away, as in it is here and readily accessible for those who wish to evolve & ascend.

Mermaids also symbolize beauty, charm, seduction and allure, and the divine feminine. Both romantic and sexual and platonic expressions of beauty and the divine feminine. This dream symbol is asking Pisces to get in tune with their inner feminine qualities. The planet Venus is exalted in Pisces, meaning Venus traits can be looked towards for integration and embodiment. Venus is the planet of pleasure, beauty, sensuality, female sexuality, and wealth. People with strong Venus energy are deeply sensual, intuitive, romantic and lovers of sexual expression with an emotional & psychological, and/or spiritual, bond. Feminine "yin" power links to mermaids appearing in dreams. Are you connected to your source of magnetic feminine power, or not? Other feminine qualities include being nurturing, empathic, receptive, passive or introverted, magnetic, caring, and having a vivid inner life. Magic relating to the water element can be enhanced too. There's an unrivaled sense of beauty associated with mermaids which leads to positive manifestation and magnetic charm. Opportunities for connections, abundance, and community are associated with the mermaid. Also, freedom and independence, particular in relation to one's sensuality and sexuality. Rebellious spirit, free-spiritedness, and open-mindedness are connected to the energetic symbolism of the mermaid. Other powers include channeling their raw and infinite potential into creativity, imagination, spirituality and psychic self-development. Using feminine sexuality is an empowering and helpful way, such as through educating others and inspiring through wisdom, spoken word, music, writing, teaching, or the like, is integral to the mermaid.

Mermaids are ultimately a reflection. They teach purity and positive mirroring, i.e. seeing everyone as a reflection and the soul or spirit that is inside. The receptive, reflective and magnetic energy transferred through a mermaid's eyes teaches mankind, regardless of their gender, true love and soulmate energy. Source is limitless, eternal, and infinite and this divine spark of creation and intuitive power is accessible when we open up to the emotional, subtle, and astral waters of the metaphysical world. Color, imagination, and artistry in addition to musical and creative talents of all kinds are connected to the mermaid. Love, beauty, elusiveness, sexual independence, self-sovereignty, mystery, allure, sensuality and emotion is what Pisces can access.

## Fairytale Characters

Other mythical creatures from Disney, fairy tales or stories find their way into their dream world frequently. Pisces doesn't see these as fantasy or separate from reality. Pisces understands that *every* idea, thought, image, theme, character/being, concept and belief is centered around one fundamental truth: the truth that everything is possible. Everything will either exist on the material plane, as embraced and accepted by our physical reality, or on some spiritual, subtle or subconscious field. Anything unseen or invisible is just as real to a Pisces as the mundane, material, or tangible. Common fairytale characters include princesses and princes, queens and kings, fairies, elves, goblins, fairy godmothers, mermaids, warriors, and other magical beings like witches, wizards, dwarves, etc.

Let's break these down:-

- *Princesses & Princes*: Princesses and princes show the part of us that needs to mature, grow up and be healed. To dream of a princess/prince is to see inside your subconscious mind and shadow self, to learn that you are currently operating from a self-righteous and self-entitled space. They're not quite Queens or Kings, they're still young and have much learning to do. The princess or prince may be a representation of a young, teenage, or young adult Pisces' shadow self and flaws or follies. It suggests immaturity but still being on the path to royalty, nobleness, and self-empowerment.
- *Queens & Kings*: Queens and kings in dreams represent a Pisces' journey to enlightenment, maturity, spiritual alignment, and self-empowerment. These dream or fairytale characters show how one has or is stepping into self-leadership and personal authority. And, accessing unique talents and gifts. Queens and kings are the ascended or higher vibrational, wiser and "leveled up" versions of princesses and princes. They suggest one has much more knowledge and self-awareness and has grown through various life lessons & cycles. Royalty, timeless wisdom, profound intuition, heightened senses and self-awareness, and a recognition of abundance as a birthright come with queens and kings. Also, a connection to the Higher Self and divine sources of inspiration.
- *Fairies and Elves*: Fairies and elves represent magic. Because Pisces is the most spiritual sign with advanced gifts naturally, this means dreaming of these symbols/characters implies they are in tune with- or being asked to connect to psychic, intuitive and imaginative gifts. Spiritual insight, divine wisdom and telepathy can be associated here. There are mystical and deeply spiritual aspects to fairies and elves. Fairies also represent innocence. Fairies show us our desires for play and self-expression relating to the inner child. Spiritual alignment too. Elves symbolize magic and nature, the spirit of forests, oceans, lakes, mountains, and caves.
- *Goblins*: Goblins show Pisces their mischievous side, either how they're accessing it or not, and what they need to do to heal and balance certain areas of their life; or aspects of their personality. They're either seen as a mischievous and playful (although annoying) spirit or an evil and bad elf. Goblins can represent a joker energy if they're not shown in an evil way. The message? Get in touch with your playful and fun-loving side, and be more light-hearted and humorous (the same applies for seeing an elf).
- *Fairy Godmothers*: Fairy godmothers have a grandmother type of energy. They

can show Pisces the power of feminine energy, ancient wisdom, and lessons and teachings acquired through time, through the maturity of age. Timeless wisdom is a symbol of fairy godmothers. They bring the energy of magic and mentorship, a "wise elder" spirit with ancient and ancestral knowledge. And, they symbolize wish fulfillment and dreams coming true through accepting personal power and learning through life's many teachings.

- *Other magical beings*: Wizards, witches and other positive magical beings are all here to remind one of their connection to spirit, in varying ways. Wizards represent magic and manifestation linked to masculine energy and the Higher Self, while witches represent intuition, sacred and divine law, and magnetism rooted in sensuality and feminine magic. Both are here to remind you of the Soul, your soul, and spiritual energy permeating the universe. Powers of communication, listening, manifestation, attraction and other Universal Laws, wisdom and evolved intuition are available with witches and wizards. Based on the dream context, their presence shows you what steps you need to take or changes you must make to align with your Higher Self and Spirit, and live up to your highest potential.
- *Warriors:* Warriors and female warrior characters show mystical and sensitive Pisces their inner strength. These dream characters often show themselves when Pisces has become too receptive, passive, or people-pleasing; self-sacrificing and feminine too. Warrior energy is primarily masculine and very self-assertive. They're connected to the primal power of Mars, and navigate life and their missions with passion, energy and vitality. Warriors have immense confidence and belief in themselves in addition to strong boundaries, self-respect, and a commitment to their goals & path. A younger or directionless Pisces can learn from this.

## Emotional Bonds

Emotions and relationships are very significant in the dreamspace for a Pisces. This is both a sign and a theme, but because the next section is so in depth I've decided to put this here. Despite all their spiritual, psychic, imaginative and creative gifts, Pisces will always be ruled by their emotions. They're a water sign, so emotions and internal feelings drive them. It is a type of core level programming. Pisces feels out situations and people before committing to something (or someone), but their primary need is based around intimacy and connection. A Pisces with strong emotional and psychological bonds in the world is like a single little fish lost at sea. People are a mirror to them, they reflect Pisces' health, well-being, emotions, beliefs, philosophies, and how far they've come on their journey of understanding and self-evolution. Intimacy is formed from the adaptable and surrendering qualities of their element, therefore the condition of relationships in dreams shows the amount of your water and subsequent "vibratory frequency." Too much water can result in excessive crying, mood swings, low moods, depression, excessive sleep, lethargy and laziness, over-indulgence, and communication problems in close relationships. And blocked or repressed emotions, an inability to express your true feelings, and a disconnection from your truth, personal ideologies, and inspiration. All of these are displayed in the dreamspace through interactions with people from real-life or dream characters.

In addition, emotions will come out in sporadic bursts and chaotic ways with too much water, such as through losing your temper in a whirlwind of emotional chaos, or acting irrationally "blurting" out all of your feelings. You may be able to express your emotions but it will be destructive and non-self serving. This shows you're avoiding the 'yang' energies of life, the Sun directly, or the other elements. Staying connected to the Moon and night's energies and only the lunar/yin forces of the world can result in a lack of passion. Also, action associated with the Sun, willpower, action and self-confidence. Pisces needs to take note of how much yin or water they are embodying. Fortunately, their subconscious mind works closely with them, so dream signs that even appear "negative" are in fact a positive push towards healing and self-mastery. Alternatively, not enough water and dreams will show emotional discord or disconnect in interactions with others. There's a lack of your natural talents in empathy, sensitivity to others' needs and health, and the ability to see beyond the surface (relating to nurturing and care). Kindness and generosity may also decrease when water is low. Dream scenarios & scenes reflect too much or not enough water, and obviously show Pisces when there is just the right amount or perfect levels.

*To increase the water element*: drink lots of water, spend time near bodies of water (rivers, lakes, streams, oceans etc.), work with the water element in meditation, engage in psychic & spiritual development exercises, and seek to strengthen your *intuition*. Meditating on or visualizing the colors purple, violet, and indigo are ideal for strengthening your intuitive mind and self. All blues work wonders for communication related to emotions and inner moods/currents. Further, anything that helps to connect you to your empathic, caring and nurturing side, such as caretaking, elderly or animal companion, volunteering or charity work (including environmental and eco help- not just animals and people!), enhances the water element within. Remember that water represents receptivity, depth of feeling, emotions, empathy and all nurturing qualities relating to care and a sense of comfort; how protected and secure you feel in your own body, and the world around. "Nesting" at home- simple resting and taking sufficient time for relaxation & rejuvenation- are ways to heal and balance water too. Watery foods like cucumbers, lettuces, fruits and organic juices, or lemon, mint or lime water, are effective options (for increasing water, and thus balancing out the other elements... Too much fire, earth or air, for example).

All in all, your primal desire and drive for deep emotional bonds including connection, intimacy, and authenticity in relationships, shows how you interact with the world. And, how you feel about yourself. Referring back to "just the right amount" or "perfect" levels of water, this is represented in dreams by positive dream scenarios and experiences. You, as a Pisces, will clearly feel joy and great pleasure in the connections shown in the dreamspace. Experiences such as community connection, interacting with kindred spirits who share a *soulful resonance*, are common in Pisces who are emotionally content and balanced (in waking life). Community and the joy of human spirit and connection reflects a positive self-image, and a balanced internal state. Love and romance are taken to new heights with many Pisces as well. Soul union and tantric forms of love, connection and sex, or polyamory, are not uncommon for spiritual and all-embracing Pisces. Picturing yourself with a lover or soulmate, engaged in conscious sex and love-making, portrays a deep-seated need for love. Emotions are generally considered healthy and flowing when this is envisioned. You possess the most evolved and advanced instincts and unconditional love. You operate on heightened and evolved emotional frequencies.

# Chapter 3: PATTERNS & SYNCHRONICITIES

## Key Dream Themes

Let's expand on some of what is already covered. Pisces is most prone to prophetic and visionary dreams, precognitive dreams predicting world events and future scenarios in their personal lives. They often see aliens, light beings, angels, witches and wizards, magical fairytale characters, and blurred or spacey dreams simply to show them how mystical the universe and dreamspace is. Pisces sign is ruled by the planet of illusion. This means reality can be distorted, they can give into self-delusion or fantasy, believing fiction is in fact true. Being so clairvoyant and clairsentient and audient means some evolved Pisces can also hear things from other dimensions. An overly logical or spiritually disconnected person may call this schizophrenia or hallucinations, yet- to the spiritually aware and psychic Pisces on a path of healing, they know better. Reality is distorted in dreams too, so some are quite literally "blurs." Consciousness observing itself, the dreamer being an onlooker and alternating between various characters or existing in the ether and empty spaces. From a different perspective, they can flow between reality effortlessly and take on a number of roles and identities, and tune into a number of dream messages and subconscious jewels of wisdom. Everything is relative to a Pisces. One can be an onlooker and main dream character at the same time, which is pretty rare! Consciousness and lucid exist simultaneously.

This gift might decrease from age 29- 30, when Pisces is stepping into self-responsibility and finding their place in the physical world, but their astral powers and strong sense of mysticism are still present. The same is true for *all* the mystical and otherworldly dream symbols, signs and themes, in fact. A person's Saturn Return occurs at around age 29, and Pisces' can hit them pretty hard. Saturn Return, to quickly digress, is when Saturn makes its journey back to the same point in your chart as it was when you were born. This happens every 29- 30 years. So, the first Saturn Return happens at age 29- 30. Saturn is symbolic of cosmic lessons, the 'big' lessons and teachings aimed to make us struggle. Saturn represents hardship and setbacks, limitations and restrictions, and also maturity and self-responsibility. This planet is also known as "Father Time" or the "Lord of Karma," and he (masculine planet) can bring out our mature adult selves. Growth, failures and disappointments are almost certainly guaranteed- and with this comes facing physical reality, but lessons and level-ups are always the result. In terms of physical reality, this is referring to practicalities, finances, career, and self-autonomy, and releasing codependency and becoming your own caregiver and provider, in other words. As Pisces can be deeply codependent and overly-emotional this is a massive lesson for them.

Thus, mystical and ethereal dreams will be strong apart from significant periods of physical and practical growth. The universe asks soulful and spiritually enlightened Pisces to take a mini break from spirituality and psychic gifts growth, and work on career, finances, and duties and practicalities in the physical world. Roots and foundations, security and physical structures (for which soul gifts and talents can shine!). Saturn Return hits us a few years before it occurs, so from around age 27 (ish). Its effects can last until 33, and the main message is that everyone is asked to look at their karma and past actions up until this stage in their life. This sensitive sign is being given a break to examine aspects and life themes they would usually neglect, all so they can step into self-sovereignty and self-empowerment. Balancing the mental, emotional, physical and spiritual bodies, and harmonizing and unifying mind, body & spirit. It can be very easy for Pisces to get lost in fantasy and dream worlds, or to neglect their financial and physical life; however, Saturn comes along to provide a necessary wake up call.

**Dream Themes during a Saturn Return (Age 28- 30)**

To start, can I just say there is a reason why I instinctively didn't complete this book until 2021. A Dream book on my own sign is something I have been intending and doing behind the scenes work for all throughout my twenties. But, it never felt fully right. My intuition always said I needed to wait a little longer, 'now wasn't the right time…' I wouldn't have understood why before however now I do. Things I understand and feel fully with all my senses and body, I couldn't have foresaw. I wouldn't have believed and thus I didn't have the wisdom or knowledge to share this.

The actual Saturn return happens at age 29- 30, but 3 years before and after are impacted as well.

Saturn Return is a wake up call. It's a time to grow up and get real. Dreams start to reflect everything Pisces has been denying, rejecting or repressing. Key practical and material necessities such as a personal income, a career or grounded path (professional, vocational or service-wise) become prominent in the dream space. The overly mystical or otherworldly dreams usually experienced are replaced by dreams centered around relationships, spiritual growth, shadow lessons, and cycles or memories in need of integration. Karma is real and comprehended on a grounded, earthly level. Instead of just dreaming about karmic exchanges and the philosophy or energetic, abstract and theoretical awareness of them, one starts to understand it on an instinctual and real-world level. Memories and experiences that once had a shadowy blur or mystical edge around them are seen on totally different levels. Consciousness gets a level up. Essentially, aspects of practical reality, waking life and the self are finally seen for the first time. If one has been denying the importance of having an income and financial independence, their subconscious mind will show this to them. If they've been too codependent, perhaps unconsciously codependent also, they will finally start to realize their follies. The previous shield or block covering their flaws and follies will become lifting a few years prior to the actual Saturn Return.

It's also a time to "choose a path." Get grounded with a decision. This may be difficult at first as indecisiveness is one of Pisces' major flaws, but hopefully significant steps no matter how small were taken during their 20s. Any helpful action towards self-healing and wholeness gets absorbed and remains in one's subconscious. Even if the lesson takes years to fully integrate, it strikes a chord and lingers positively contributing to their aura and energy field. So, later in life it is easier accessible. Saturn (Return) provides a second or even third chance, an opportunity to try again and do things over- this time at a higher vibration. Being practical and mature isn't the same as devolving spiritually. Spiritual illumination and the journey towards enlightenment, cosmic consciousness, etc. is synergistic with grounding spirit and spirituality into the material realm. An integral lesson for Pisces is to fully understand that they are humans having a spiritual experience and spirit having a human experience, simultaneously. Think back to the Pisces glyph of the two fish…. one ascends and one descends, spirit and matter are connected through a bridge or cord. One's consciousness is the bridge.

So, dreams at this time will always reflect change and transformation, growth and practical and financial transitions. As the 'Lord of Karma' this time period through the subconscious mind in dreams asks you to examine your history and past. A light is shone into what you've mastered and what you haven't, where you've won and where you've failed. Getting real with yourself takes honesty. Patterns of victimhood can also be discovered and overcome during a Saturn Return. Discipline, determination and perseverance will be uncovered and analyzed, and if you've been slacking or not living up to your full potential dreams will portray what your Higher Self wants from you. We all have a destiny, a unique soulprint... Saturn Return is a wake up call to your true self and service. Personal and professional manifestation will reveal itself while epiphanies through astral visions and dreams showing hidden things, such as attitudes, beliefs, emotions, escapist tendencies and self-denial, and when you truly shine, will be known. Reaping what you sow is another main theme and endings lead to rebirth and alchemical transformation. Saturn teaches responsibility and the true meaning of duty, to look within and "show up for yourself;" be completely transparent and evolve past the Piscean need to escape or run. Running from true feelings and the pain and heartache that comes with life is essential in order to manifest success and self-alignment on the earth plane. Whether it's relating to love, relationships, beliefs, financial losses, heartache and death, separation and big life challenges, the age of your Saturn Return can be a blessing if one chooses to work consciously with their dreams.

If female you might start to dream of pregnancy, or being surrounded by lots of children. OR potentially teaching them. Pisces loves the playful and innocent energy of children, Neptune rules innocence and naivety, after all; the innocence we feel in youth. In late twenties Pisces tends to experience more family dreams either of starting their own family or teaching children, having children, or choosing a path involving children and family. Or, dreams will feature various scenes of work, career and self-leadership, self-autonomy and new found power and authority. If one is in a creative, performing or artistic career path, or on their way to getting there, they will likely see themselves embodying a vibration of stardom. Pisces has the potential to become a wayshower, inspirational person, shining star or even famous person. Having such unique creative and imaginative gifts makes them a force to be reckoned, if and when they embrace their path and purpose. Stepping into self-leadership with the masculine assertion required is a key step towards alignment. The spaced out, overly compromising and adaptable, and indecisive ways of their past no longer cuts it. Lacking focus and grounding are two major things that prevent them achieving true happiness and abundance in life, and it can take all the years of twenties to their early, mid or even late 30s to recognize this. Dreams will portray their deep burning desire to step into the spotlight and connect to their gifts and unique abilities, to inspire, educate and raise humanity's vibration.

If they are destined to become a powerful and respected healer, shaman, or therapist or counselor in their community, dreams will also show this. The subconscious mind works to show Pisces whatever lessons and teachings they have been slowly acquiring throughout their youth and early adult years. Some people step right into their path, others have a glimpse and taste of life to come, at around 21- 24 (on average) before finally realizing the power and self-worth they hold when Saturn Return hits. They may see themselves as an elder or shaman in the center of a circle, respected by their community with people coming to them for wisdom and insight. They may picture themselves healing others or offering workshops or therapies at a festival, surrounded by colors and the vibrancy of a 'rainbow community' culture. Pisces is a bohemian at heart, a free-spirit regardless of how mature, wise and grounded they become. Traditional 9 to 5 jobs which further don't reflect their passions are unlikely. Pisces need community, kindred spirits and a life with soul, passion, cosmic or spiritual energy, and activities and actions that mirror their deep need for intimate connections and healing. Even Pisces who do choose a more "left brain" job- IT, politics, marketing, technology or science, etc. will envision themselves in new positions of self-authority and leadership. A Pisces' magnetic personality will always radiate; their primary instinctual driving force in life is *connection*. This can reflect into modeling, acting, graphic design and other similar jobs too.

Inspiration, motivation, hard-work and determination are keywords for the dream themes of 28- 33. Practical affairs might start to be merged with spirituality and the 'mystical vibe' of their youth once life lessons have been integrated. Saturn is, ultimately, the wise old man and elder who sees through your self-deception, illusions and excuses. Even pain and loss that is a truly life-changing experience will be given a dose of practical wisdom and awareness. And, some wise old souls who made solid choices and chose to commit to their path early on will feel just how powerful their true potential is. If this is the case, Saturn Return provides information and reassurance: *"you chose well, this is your path, you're powerful and self-sovereign; own up to it!"* Not all relationships, marriages or careers are meant to break. In this sense, it is a sort of "rights of passage," embracing one's destiny and future legacy, and a maturation phase of authentication. A call to discipline and utmost self-honesty is in divine order and the practical dreamer energy of Pisces is tested.

**It's all an Illusion**

Continuing on from before we digressed, throughout life dreams will always have a strong element of fantasy. Illusion and distortion allow for flexibility and adaptability in the dreamspace. Being an observer or onlooker and dream character, main or secondary, is a rare gift. It not only allows the dreamer (Pisces) to explore and gain access to a range of emotions, impressions, and subconscious insights, but also many deeper meanings into the mystery of the universe, and dream worlds themselves. Pisces can walk through walls, communicate with animals, read minds, swim underwater, and fly. Flying, breathing underwater, and communicating with animals are very significant. They reflect hidden gifts and abilities unbeknown to a large percentage of mankind. See, there are multiple dimensions of consciousness, many planes of being. For a Pisces, reality is an illusion and there is so much more than a physical realm. If you've ever had an out of body experience (OBE) or astrally projected you will know what I mean. OBE's and astral projection (or astral travel) are some of the "foundation" experiences of the realm of lucidity and multidimensionality. Nothing is real yet everything is real- nothingness and everythingness is a philosophy Pisces embraces. It then provides doorways or portals for growth, subconscious and metaphysical insight, and advanced dream abilities. Illusion and fantasy are pretty interchangeable for many Pisces… positively, this gives rise to self-evolution as portrayed through a range of extrasensory and divine gifts.

Waking life and dream worlds merge into one which leads to the healing gifts and shamanic dream abilities as explored later. Defying the law of nature is common. Regardless of whether we want to label this as reality or fantasy, fact or fiction, there is always a symbolic insight or greater truth present. Recognizing *its all an illusion* lets Pisces *transcend* illusion, ascending to new heights within and around. They take the wisdom and insight learned from the dreams and then apply it to real-time. All sorts of amazing dream experiences and revelations are available through Neptune's influence…. Shapeshifting is a common trait for people born into this sign- they may experience dreams as an animal, specifically animals linked to Shamanism and cosmic healing energies (more on this later). Shapeshifting also occurs between human characters. Pisces is so multi-dimensional and adaptable that they can teleport and change form, travel through atoms and portals, and bounce between worlds and timelines. If anyone is going to explain how time travel is real, and give you an understandable explanation of it, it would be Pisces. Lucidity is a natural state and phenomena like astral travel, astral projection, and shamanic dreaming feature strongly throughout childhood, teenage years and early adult life. Being so empathic too allows them to enter into unseen and usually inaccessible worlds through *emotion*. Emotion is a force, and Pisces has mastered it.


**The Artist, Poet, and Inspirational Visionary (Practical Dreamers)**

It is assumed that water signs are simply sensitive, emotional and kind and nurturing. Many people believe the fire signs are the ones with the musical, artistic and creative gifts, but *Pisces* embodies an evolved and higher vibration of all the abilities you see in the fire signs. They are natural poets, writers, musicians, artists, entertainers, performers, speakers, actors and creatives. Any creative and artistic skill you can think of- Pisces is capable of being the best in their field! It's important that they apply themselves. Being a *practical dreamer* is directly linked to their ability to step into their talents and develop them to the best standard. As the Dreamer of the Zodiac (unique dream symbol), Pisces is able to connect to the unlimited & infinite realms of creative potential and imagination. Dreamy, astral, subtle, ethereal and spiritual qualities are available to them. The other angle is lacking boundaries and being so impressionable, or adaptable, that they lose sight of their dreams. It is easy for Pisces to fall into apathy and idleness or simply not make use of their time and talents. Instead of being a practical dreamer they then remain in the shadows and shadow worlds of the dreamspace. Something to be mindful of, at the very least.

Fortunately, there's so much boundless imaginative potential that they usually heal from this, and quite quickly. Pisces can slip into a variety of roles. There are often two different versions of you within- no, not a negative personality disorder, it's something you're fully aware of and quite enjoy. You can alternate between the helpless romantic or sensitive vulnerable being in need of saving, or love and support; to the self-empowered God or Goddess with immense talent, confidence, and contagious optimism. In a way, as a Pisces you are like a talented actor who didn't need to go to a prestigious acting academy. Empathy runs through you so powerfully and strongly that you are *the empath*, the psychic, intuitive and deeply emotive healer and visionary who 'envisions' new worlds and realities. And, can connect to unseen invisible energy, information, and emotions & beliefs. Senses are extraordinary in self-evolved Pisces. You can tune into a huge array of human emotions, not to mention the divine or collective consciousness: superconsciousness. Subconscious forces and gifts in perception, observation, and self-awareness are fine-tuned too. Similar to sister sign Cancer, you're ruled by a feminine and subconscious mind 'associated' planet (Cancer is ruled by the Moon). This is why Pisces and Cancer and Pisces and Scorpio are considered ideal matches, in love, business, and platonic partnerships. Artistic and imaginative talents are some of your greatest strengths. Equally, you don't feel yourself when you're blocked or limited and unable to express yourself creatively, musically, or artistically.

Due to your opposite sign being Virgo, there is a practical and grounded magic to your artistic gifts. Some Pisces possess amazing personal power and authority, characteristics you wouldn't instantly assume with such as a sensitive and emotional sign. Pisces draws its strength from the two main qualities of Virgo, service and helpfulness. They're able to step into roles of self-leadership, personal authority, and soul alignment. Gifts and talents shine through in a grounded and modest way- there's no absence of humility or grace yet there's equal measures of rare strength. Pisces will always be introverted and feminine at the start and end of each day, but this doesn't mean they can't shine or use their voice in an outgoing way. In dreams, Pisces may envision themselves on a stage performing (singing, playing a musical instrument, entertaining people in some way) or letting their inner creative genius out to play. Virgo's influence as their opposite enables them to channel any higher dimensional or imaginative energies & frequencies into the earth plane. Inspiration is strong and Pisces shares the down-to-earth and sensual loving qualities of earth. Do note though, younger Pisces may be prone to rejecting the grounded aspects of life. They believe themselves to be "above" the earth plane and duties (to self and others) of the earth plane.

### Love, Soulmates, and Kindred Spirits

Soulmates are a key feature of Pisces' life and journey. This spiritual and "wanderlusty" sign is open to alternative love affairs and arrangements. Bisexuality, demisexuality, sapiosexuality, asexuality/celibacy and polyamory are all common. Let's quickly run through these.

- *Bisexuality*: Many Pisces choose to be bisexual primarily based on the duality of life. They recognize life involves yin and yang, that there are feminine and masculine energies within everything and everyone, and that the main goal of life is to find a balance and unity. Thus, they choose to embrace both sexes because it aligns with their primary philosophy in life: *Oneness, interconnectedness, and indiscrimination*.
- *Demisexuality*: This is pretty much the Pisces personality. Demisexuality is only feeling attracted to someone when they have an *emotional bond*. This is enhanced even further if someone has their Sun and Venus and/or Moon in Pisces. A Pisces' world is tied into emotional connection… It is no wonder that many Pisceans are naturally demisexual!
- *Sapiosexuality*: Sapiosexuality is feeling sexually attracted through *intelligence*. It's all about a psychological and intellectual or philosophical connection. This is common in Pisces with an air sign as their Rising/Ascendant and/or Moon. For example, Pisces Sun with Gemini, Libra or Aquarius Rising (Ascendant) will naturally feel attracted to people with advanced cerebral gifts. Intellect, a bright and inventive or innovative mind, and fine-tuned perception all fall into this category.
- *Asexuality or Celibacy:* Pisces frequently go through bouts of conscious celibacy, 'aka' asexuality. They choose to refrain from sexual union to focus on spiritual growth and *soul alignment*. Pisces recognizes that we all come into this life alone and leave this world alone simultaneously. Being a "lone wolf" to engage in self-mastery and self-development is not uncommon. There are no sexual desires when one is focusing on the higher self and subsequent connections that form. Asexuality and celibacy are a type of self-conditioning, one programs their mind, thoughts and emotions through their overall *energetic blueprint*, or *energetic vibratory frequency*, to interact with people on a certain wavelength. By making conscious choices to abstain from sexual play and union, Pisces is able to access subtle dimensions and connect with others emotionally, spiritually and

mentally/psychologically.

- *Polyamory*: Polyamory is having multiple lovers, entering into a type of "free love" situation, or conscious and ethical non-monogamy. Pisces loves to love, but they are equally undiscriminating, non-jealous, tolerant and all-embracing.

Soulmates and kindred spirits feature often and strongly. Music and other forms of imaginative expression are portrayed with lovers, soulmates or kindred spirits. Pisces loves community and needs to feel part of something "greater," something "higher" and transcendental. This implies transcendence of the ego. Divinity shines through in dreams as does tantric intimacy and sexual union. Being a Mutable (adaptable) sign enables Pisces to tune into every and any aspect of consciousness, and expand it in their mind, dreams and lives. Pisces accesses a higher power simply to birth something new into the world. They're similar to Aquarius in this respect and Aquarius is the *Water*-bearer, the sign just before Pisces; their ancient ruler is Jupiter, making them connected to higher ideals, philosophy, spirituality and the lifelong pursuit of knowledge. To 'know thyself' is the Pisces sign in embodiment. Virgo, the sign of duty, helpfulness, purity and service, is Pisces' opposite, and with this truth comes the awareness that they are supposed to find balance with Virgo's strengths. Relating to love this symbolizes purity, soul deep love on a higher plane or frequency. It's Pisces' desire to transcend toxicity including karmic cycles, to meet partners and soulmates on the best possible vibration.

Pisces wants to merge, bond and experience ecstatic bliss of sexual and intimate union. Their partners are a mirror of them to find truth and learning, Pisces grows through their significant others. Being the least jealous sign of the Zodiac, Pisces can often encourage people close to them, who resonate with the highly independent and free-spirited vibe, to enter into a conscious non-monogamous or 3-way partnership. This isn't suggesting Pisces is unfaithful, Pisces is incredibly loyal and devoted when in a relationship. Faithfulness is one of their strengths. However, the journey there will be full of love affairs and experimentations in love, and some choose to adopt polyamory as their lifelong choice. Whatever their preference, dreams will show them where they're currently operating (vibrating, their energetic frequency and current belief system) and their emotional needs in love. This is a major dream theme because it is highly unlikely for a Pisces to not ever have dreams rooted around love and connection. They'll either be shown insight into their past, past exes and love affairs, etc., or guidance on their future- like a precognitive dream or vision of a future lover, romantic situation, or partnership to be expected.

Even the dreams not rooted around love and intimacy provide insight into their emotional desires and mindset around companionship. I.e. dreaming of stepping into self-leadership and thriving in a career, or as their own boss, portrays that they are feeling extremely independent and content within their own being. Dreaming of being high-spirited and on the road, traveling and connected to their adventure-loving side shows they are aligned with their higher self and talents, so a committed partnership is not in the forefront of their consciousness at this time.

## The Victim-Martyr-Rescuer Complex

This is a key dream theme that runs throughout early life, specifically until they have healed their wounds and integrated essential life lessons. Pisces is ruled by the 12th house in astrology, the house of dreams, secrets and emotions- and intuitive, psychic and spiritual gifts. Everything "unseen," mystical and unconscious relates to this house. Despite all of Pisces' positive traits & gifts, they are still open to the victim-martyr-rescuer or savior complex. This is a not so holy trinity. It can influence all aspects of their life and lead to depression, melancholy and illusion if not careful or mindful. This is closely linked to the shadow self or personality, the part of us that is considered undesirable, impure or dark. The shadow self are the things we would prefer to deny, reject, or repress. It is through repression and denial, however, where we give into the things we do not wish to embody. What we resist, persists. So, playing victim or rescuer/savior, or becoming a martyr, is something Pisces needs to heal to step into their soul gifts and talents. Because Pisces is so emotionally advanced and seeks connection in life, sex and intimacy can be a tricky subject. Pain is experienced in an almost unbearable way for many Pisces, they take on the worlds' and other people's suffering. It can be intense and being the empath of the Zodiac makes them feel things just that little bit more deeply than anyone else.

Sex, instincts, and a strong need for intimacy are all tied into one another. Sometimes the only way out is through, and this is something Pisces needs to come to terms with. They may choose to avoid certain truths or push things below the surface, back to the world of illusion and mysticism (where suffering is glamorized and made into a 'holy act'). I certainly did this in my youth and early adult years. In pursuit of the Higher Self and abilities related to the higher chakras, Pisces will often reject or neglect their lower chakras. The shadow self personality is deeply emotional, primal, instinctive and vulnerable; it is linked to the lower two chakras- the Root and Sacral, the energy centers associated with sex, reproduction, security, survival instincts, emotions, and complete openness and intimacy in interpersonal relationships. When your shadow self has taken over and not in a healthy way such as through creative power, as the shadow also links to emptiness, creative potential and unlimited power, one is weak and vulnerable. Boundaries are weakened, which is something super-sensitive Pisces has issues with anyway. Instincts can lead to intuition and qualities connected to the third eye (Higher Self/Mind), but first we must go through our shadow and sexual desires. Instinctive needs for connection, bonding and intimacy- both platonic and sexual or on the "soul-merging" vibe- are integral to everyone's journey. Being mystical or open to the world of subtle and spiritual energy and dreams doesn't excuse Pisces from the fact that they were born into a body.

Victimhood takes over when one denies, represses, or rejects for too long. When we push everything below the surface we reject self-responsibility. We aren't able to take ownership of our emotions or feelings, or our life, and therefore hidden insecurities and resentments build up. Over time, this leads to something known as *unconscious projection*. One unconsciously projects all their "stuff"- internal shadow things and insecurities, at others. It can lead to vicious cycles of codependency, ungroundedness, and depression or melancholy if left unchecked for long periods of time. Pisces is lucky in that they can find a temporary fix. They can access the dream, subconscious, or imaginative worlds for arguably amazing and extraordinary expressions, creativity, extrasensory gifts of perception, etc. But, one day they will have to face the music and return to the issues floating just below the surface. They have to 'do the work,' the shadow and healing work. Playing victim is not something Pisces likes to admit, mainly due to the fact that they are selfless and supremely compassionate. Pisces will fight for an underdog or exhibit advanced levels of courage and devotion when standing up for other people, or animals and the planet itself. Yet when it comes to their own well-being, they don't treat themselves with the same kindness. Victimhood serves no one, it actually takes away from their power and independence (things that are deeply important to them). Being a victim then gives into martyrdom. Martyrdom is essentially being persecuted or shamed and "killed" (metaphorically speaking, for Pisces) due to their beliefs, spiritual vibration, and soul.

Then, the need to rescue or save others takes over. Duality defines Pisces, they're creatures of duality and therefore extremes. All we have to do is look at a Pisces' love life to confirm this! One moment, they will be floating from lover to lover, completely at one with their free-spirited, polyamorous, and wanderlust vibe and self. The next they will be craving soul-deep love and monogamy. They can quite literally slip from two apparent extremes within a few breaths, hours, days, or weeks. This innate tendency towards extremes makes them succumb to taking on the role of the savior or rescuer. They're naturally inspiring, so the positive aspect of this is the ability to inspire and preach in a supportive, helpful, and wise woman or man way. Pisces will always be wise and incredibly insightful. However, the victim-martyr-rescuer complex trio ultimately leads to their downfall and melancholy, confusion and the like. *The positive?* This eases up with maturity and age.

## Recurring dreams

Many Pisces report being immersed in distant worlds. They frequently visit "maze-like" dream scenarios where they have trials & tests to complete. I write this as a Pisces, but I have conversed with many evolved and spiritually open Pisces, men and women- and people of different ages. The key dreams outlined above and recurring dreams are common for almost all Pisces. There are multiple levels to a Pisces' dreamscape. Because they are ruled by *the* planet of dreams and the subconscious mind (Neptune), not to mention illusion, mysticism and spirituality, Pisces has a unique insight and glimpse into the *infinite potential* of existence. Virtually every dimension, world, plane and subtle vibration can be accessed.

There are certain dream scenes that repeat to show a lesson or offer a 'level up' in consciousness. Dreams are very much linked to evolution, self-development, and self-mastery to many Pisces. One recurring theme that I've found prominent is what I like to call the "maze dream." This is a dark one, a maze-like trial which I knew represented the psyche. I had this dream regularly from around age 14 all the way to my late teens/early twenties. I was a lesser version of myself, a creature like Gollum from Lord of Rings, but more 'horrible' looking. I was inside a brain, essentially, and I knew this brain symbolized the psyche and consciousness. Ultimately, I was going through cosmic spider webs inside this holographic brain-maze. It was dark and it was scary, and I felt weird- the vibe was very repressed and trial-like. This maze was symbolic of the various levels of consciousness within, so it was definitely a highly symbolic dream.

Basically, many Pisces have this exact or a very similar dream, a maze and/or brain/psyche/consciousness trial being the underlying theme. Dreams like this portray the cyclic nature of evolution. Recurring dreams with any "otherworldly," dark vibe and feeling is the subconscious mind (and your higher self) way of saying, 'you are on the verge of a breakthrough… great healing and level ups are available to you now.' Emotions, relationships, and your belief systems and daily feelings in waking life should be explored.

Other symbolic recurring dreams of this type include factories, houses with internal mazes, abandoned buildings, warehouses, parks and nature trails, caves, dark tunnels, underground systems, and running away from something in an open field or space. Pisces also frequently dreams of superpowers. Nature and supernatural, extrasensory, abilities of the animal queen and kingdom are where Pisces draws their insight and self-realizations. Birds show them they can fly (metaphorically and spiritually speaking), reminding them of their connection to spirit and the astral planes. Snakes show them they're psychic and eternal, also showing them their kundalini serpent power; owls represent the ability to see in the dark and connect to the shadow self and realms; and any underwater animal symbolizes their ability to 'breathe underwater,' i.e. feeling comfort in the realm of emotions and be at home in the depths of the sea (subconsciousness). Pisces has many extrasensory abilities as explored in chapter 1. Nature reminds them of their innate gifts and powers.

Recurring dreams also happen around:-

- Emotions and the shadow self
- Relationships, which mirror their soul and psyche
- Love and intimacy
- Alien lands and "strange worlds"
- Spaceships, star systems and planets
- Universe exploration
- Specific dream characters, including conversations
- Ethereal and astral energies and awareness
- Angels, ascended masters, and light beings
- Celestial transits and eclipses, interstellar alignments

Golden temples, Diamonds, Christ-like figures, crystalline structures, temples, and magical books with ancient and timeless stories to tell are core key symbols of Pisces. Pisces is able to access other worlds so they're connected to portals of cosmic, higher, divine and spiritual/mystical consciousness. The array of symbols available here is limitless. Anything considered sublime and mystical, or godly and heavenly, comes under Pisces' dreaming abilities. They become transported to distant lands… they're visited by angelic beings or light deities and entities… they sit in caves or under mountain tops and waterfalls, and see the ethereal energy surrounding nature and the natural world… they can also transcend the perceived limitations of the 3-dimensional universe, in dreams (and in waking life). Pisces' third eye is open- they're psychic and clairvoyant beyond belief, clairsentient and clairaudient too. Pisces will often hear sounds as if they're coming from another dimension. They'll see, hear, taste, smell and feel things in their dreams, and then wake up being able to recall the exact sensation. Sometimes Pisces has such amazing dreams simply to show them what is possible. Unlimited potential and infinite possibilities. A Pisces dream recall and memory is awe-inspiring. Dreams and waking life overlap for them, meaning it can sometimes be difficult to know or remember whether something occurred in a dream or in everyday reality. Mythological creatures, characters from fairytales, and divine assistance in the form of shamans, elders, fairies, light beings, angels and mermaids show themselves regularly. Reality can be confused with fantasy and fantasy certainly plays on a dreaming Pisces' mind, but- regardless- mythological and magical creatures make themselves known. All of these are cyclic dreams aimed to show Pisces their true spirit, some inner part of themselves.

The imagination of a Pisces is advanced. Neptune rules instincts, the imagination, spirituality & mysticism, and intuitive and psychic abilities, thus Pisces' dreams reflect this. But Pisces isn't just all elves and witches, unicorns and ethereal dream scenes that show the deep and ethereal/astral realms of the dreamspace...

*Prophetic and precognitive dreams* feature strongly. The capacity for transcending the limits of time and space is powerful. As a water sign, Pisces is able to access the past, present and future in a way that leads to self-realization and spiritual growth. They are open to energetic and spiritual symbolism shining a light on things they need to release, or that which relates to their past; including past cycles and chapters that no longer serve their growth or highest potential, and aspects of their current life and self. Their immediate life situation may be shown in a way that encompasses a past version of themselves and a future version simultaneously. Water signs are attuned to the frequency of *multidimensionality*. Water energy is psychic, clairvoyant and intuitive, so they can transcend any perceived limitations of a physical and material reality. Pisces is especially a master at this. Accompanying this is the vivid imagery they see. Dreams can be intensely vivid and life-like for them- dream reality is experienced with all of their senses. While air or fire may only be able to remember with their minds, potentially some instinct and sounds (air) too, Pisces can recall the scents, sounds, feelings, subtle impressions, moods, colors, tastes and images. Every single aspect of the dream can be remembered as if it were a scene from waking life. The atmosphere, mood and overall vibe of the dream is important... A lot of messages are hidden in the environment, specific characters, and the invisible message as well. It is customary to see religious symbols or ancient texts, scriptures and writings or books. Seeing angels, Christ, Buddha and sacred books portray how connected they are to spirit and the divine. These are positive dream omens steering them back to their soul and true selves.

Other positive recurring dream themes are being simply still and serene, at peace, in places of beauty. Natural landscapes, forests, jungles, beaches, temples, deserts, mountains and any and every place in the natural world shows that there is peace and tranquility in one's life. All aspects of the self seem to be balanced and this usually sensitive and emotional water sign has found a sense of 'home within' and oneness. Psychological/mental, emotional, spiritual and physical bodies are balanced and in harmony. Quiet, calm water particularly expresses harmony in their personal lives. Finally, colorful fruits represent Pisces' desire for purity and spiritual alignment. Fruits show that one is taking care of their health and that their chakras (subtle energy systems) are in harmony and working (divine) order. Fruits represent a person's "rainbow light body" as well. This is something people spiritually attuned with an open third eye understand. Meditation, spiritual practice, self-development, chakra and aura healing, and introspection can all help develop this, and activate one's *astral body*.

## Astral Travel & Projection (Pisces' natural gifts!)

Astral travel and astral projection are extremely common for Pisces, the *Old Soul* and *Dreamer*. Astral travel is the ability to leave your body when the veil is thin, so just before sleep or when one is in a deeply meditative space. Before sleep the astral realms are easily accessible, especially so for Pisces. One's mind leaves their body while still remaining connected through a cord. In astral travel, they quite literally travel, they're free to explore multiple realms and dimensions at ease. In astral projection the same initial process begins; your mind leaves your body and "projects" outwards, into the universe, the astral planes, and the spiritual dimensions. A cord is still present. But, with astral projection you remain conscious and aware of your body and the link to the earth plane. In astral projection you may experience yourself as an avatar on a different planet or in another body. You're still very much conscious of your body and life here on earth, however you're able to experience multiple planes simultaneously. From one perspective, the 'other' body, world or dimension is a projection and you are in fact human on earth, at this time. From another perspective, there is a more advanced and evolved version of you existing in a different realm, and this human earthly incarnation is a projection from your Higher Self. Think of the soul as eternal and infinite… It exists on this plane, in the earth realm, and on earth- yet it is timeless and transcends the limits (or perceived limits) of a 3-dimensional earth reality. If you can understand it like this, and as a Pisces you almost certainly do, you will see the unlimited possibilities for astral projection & astral travel.

Pisces can use the ethereal subtle, astral and spiritual realms of timelessness, multidimensionality and infinite consciousness to raise their vibration and travel, and so forth. The body becomes a portal and channel and the mind is free to wander. This means, your Higher Self becomes active, and a lot can happen and be realized when your Third Eye and Higher Self/Mind is active and awakened. Pisces as the most spiritual and evolved sign can use the subtle energy and astral realms readily accessible to "explore." New insights and extraordinary awakenings can happen in this space. One is able to see beyond the veil of illusion, learn the deepest mysteries of the universe, and connect with past lives, future lives, and everything in between. Like the event explained above, you may be a star seeded soul with a link or cord to another time, place and universe or world. Your soul may be so advanced that this lifetime, in this body in this time, is merely a vessel and conduit for a higher consciousness. We can call this your Higher Self, cosmic or super consciousness itself, or some ascended master or light being; all would be true. Reality is subjective and time and space are relative. Pisces understands that even time travel is possible, because time is not linear. When we activate our consciousness and raise our vibrations high enough so that our light bodies are operating at their highest potential, time travel becomes possible. Our conscious mind is free to leave this incarnation (physical body/vessel) and travel to a different time and space. The physical realm and our subsequent bodies are just vessels, conduits…. Thus, multiple realities and dimensions exist simultaneously or have the capacity to.

Edgar Cayce was a powerful clairvoyant who is well-known for channeling his higher self. In his words, these extraordinary channeling and astral experiences are intuitively known to him as the/his subconscious mind exploring the dream realm. It may sound too simple to be legitimate to someone who isn't Pisces, but we Pisces know this to be true. I myself, if I do say so myself, am a powerful mystic with direct links to mystical & subtle dimensions and multiple planes, where clairvoyance, higher self channeling and shamanic healing powers are rich! I have both my Sun and Venus in Pisces and a grand water trine, so this might explain why I can do some of the things I do. I know many Pisces who also have awe-inspiring dreams and astral experiences, therefore it is clear this really is a Pisces gift and skill. Pisces can merge with the divine and transcend the physical realm. Astral travel allows your mind to "wander," to float around and explore altered states of consciousness, and this can lead to profound visions and powerful imagery. Divine insight, esoteric and ancient wisdom, universal archetypes and spiritual guidance are all possible. Of course, the Higher Self and Crown chakra linking to cosmic consciousness, soul, and the Akashic Records are also accessible. The Akashic Records are something that haven't been mentioned yet. This won't appeal to all Pisces but it will to many of you.

The Akashic Records are a holographic library of all past, present and future memories and experiences. They provide wisdom unknown to most of mankind and can only be accessed by someone with an open Crown and Third Eye chakra, someone who works closely with dreams and holds a strong spiritual vibration. The Akashic Records are like a 'living library.' They're a portal into reincarnation, past lives, future lives, the time of Atlantis, ancient civilization, secrets of the universe, and knowledge relating to personal individuals' lives. Minds and souls are timelessly connected here. The Akashic Records exist on a higher plane, so they are actually always here. It is up to us to choose whether we wish to embrace their existence and tune into them for healing, insight and evolution. They originate from Hindu philosophy, with *Akasha* meaning an all-pervading etheric field, or field in the ether, which holds a record of past events. Universal events, thoughts, words, emotions, interactions, personal and global energy exchanges, and actions, from all lifeforms in the universe- not just human- are stored in the Akashic Records. Astral projection can serve as a gateway to extrasensory experiences and new pathways of consciousness exploration. A cord remains creating a bridge between your physical body to the place your mind is projecting to. If you choose to access higher wisdom and divine truth, such as the Akashic Records, consciously; this in turn strengthens your cosmic cord. This comes naturally to many Pisces however *all* Pisces can develop this gift with time and conscious effort. Being ruled by Neptune and the 12th house has many advantages.

**Binaural Beats (A Pisces' Personal Tool!)**

One thing that's helped me on my journey, yet isn't traditionally associated with Dreaming or Astrology, is the use of binaural beats at assisting dream exploration. You can use binaural beats to enhance astral travel & projection and lucid and shamanic dreaming. Also, subconscious connection and the ability to dream more vividly in general. Binaural beats are unique frequencies of sound used to alter one's consciousness. The moment they are heard and received the brain responds based on the intention or purpose of the soundwave. Each frequency range or tone has specific effects, which means they can be used for lucid dreaming and astral encounters. Binaural beats affect unconsciousness, subconsciousness, and the conscious mind. They affect inner currents, thought patterns, emotional frequencies, subtle impressions and belief systems, and everything relating to the inner you. They're essentially a form of sound therapy or sound healing. They can further release and remove unconscious blocks preventing you from accessing your higher self and full potential. Internal shifts occur and buried wounds, trauma, or detrimental and self-limiting beliefs can be eased and healed. Below are three of the best binaural beat frequencies for heightened astral experiences.

- *Gamma*: Your mind is in a natural state of high awareness, strong perception and expanded consciousness at this frequency. Transcendental awareness comes about which helps to enhance astral encounters, projection and travel.
- *Delta*: This frequency is found in sleep wave patterns and when brain activity is slow. Deep sleep links to the experiences available in astral travel.
- *Theta*: Meditation and inner peace are the main effects of theta. This one is particularly effective as the mind enters a stage of deep peace.

## Other Advanced Dream techniques

### Lucid Dreaming

Pisces are natural lucid dreamers. Lucid dreaming as you may already be aware is being conscious and aware while asleep. It's like having a torchlight on in darkness, and you are free to focus that light wherever you wish. Lucid dreaming allows your mind to wander and explore the dreamspace. It is a blissful and euphoric feeling, not dark or repressed like some of the otherworldly experiences and opportunities for shadow work integration. Lucid dreaming can be healing, it is just generally associated with being in the light- in lightness. Lucidity is a state of clarity and perception, complete clear sight. In saying this, shadow work healing and integration can come about. When one lucid dreams they enter a state of awareness, the dreamer becomes they are dreaming and, with time and practice, can control the direction of their (lucid) dreams. Dream characters, narrative, themes, environments and virtually every aspect of the dream can be understood and further controlled. A dream-initiated lucid dream (DILD) is where something within the dream triggers you as the dreamer to become lucid, while a wake-initiated lucid dream (WILD) is more conscious, i.e. one moves from waking to dreaming with no loss of awareness. In WILD you slip into lucidity and holistic awareness effortlessly, or at least consciously.

Lucid dreaming manifestations in Pisces:-

- Awareness of the dream state and orientation.
- Awareness of memory function- memory is often whole and clear,

intact.

- Awareness of the self, psyche and soul.
- Awareness of the capacity to be in control and make decisions.
- Awareness of dream meanings, messages and environments.
- Awareness of self-awareness itself; clarity and subjective perception.

What's even more fascinating and adds to the already long list of Piscean traits and characteristics, is how people born into the sign of the Fish can communicate with other people in the dreamspace. I remember this very vivid experience with a Pisces friend of mine. We were both majorly on the lucid dreaming vibe, both eating healthy and keeping our light bodies pure. We also had a close spiritual and emotional connection… I had a dream within a dream within a dream (process this). ~ 'A dream within a dream, within another dream.' I was woken up by my friend saying- through the ether and astral realm; "Grace, wake up. Wake up!" My alarm actually went off a couple of minutes before it did in waking life (in the first dream) so I woke up into the second dream within the dream. I thought I was awake initially, my astral self got out of bed and I had a vision of fruit and colors, the colors of the rainbow. Then, I finally woke up, into my physical body. There were multiple layers and my light/astral/spiritual body was vibrating powerfully, very powerfully. Clearly so was my friend's as he was able to communicate with me in the dream space. We had practiced telepathy a few times together (in waking life), sending it eachother colors and shapes to receive psychically. So there was a deep bond there. The message I knew and felt instinctively was that I need to eat just fruit in order to access such evolved spiritual gifts. The thing about the dreamspace and extrasensory astral abilities such as this is one must be vibrating at a high frequency, and this isn't possible with dense foods.

**We explore this topic in depth, in addition to real multidimensional and "magical" experiences of my own in my later book, a complete record of my dreams from youth. (I have kept a dream diary from 2012 all the way up to adulthood, rich in vivid dream symbolism blessed to me from Spirit…)**

*Interesting facts*

The Hindu practice of Yoga Nidra involves consciously dreaming, so they cultivate the ability to be aware and lucid. Tibetan Buddhists also have a similar practice and call it Dream yoga. These practices have been around for thousands of years. Ancient Greeks were also lucid dreaming and engaging in advanced dream techniques, as were Egyptians. Ancient Egyptians had dream temples where people would go to sleep to receive insights and wisdom from their dreams. Aristotle and Galen (ancient Greece) both wrote significant texts on lucid dreaming and its power.

## Shamanic Dreaming

There are two signs that are natural shamans. These are Pisces and Scorpio, two of the most magnetically and instinctively powerful, psychic, intuitive, clairvoyant, clairsentient, clairaudient, and telepathy capable signs. Many Pisces start to awaken to spiritual gifts intuitively. This means, they don't have to read a book or receive healing or shamanic attunement from an elder or master! Pisces is so connected to Spirit and the astral realms that they float freely into the shadow and shamanic lands, realms, etc. The shadow and shamanic realms are intrinsically linked, as a shamanic guide, healer and channel draws their power from the darkness, from the subconscious and astral realms. Shamanic masters and practitioners also need to go on their own journey of healing before being a channel for others. To master the light, one must first master their inner darkness. You won't find a true shamanic healer or master who hasn't undertaken a lifelong or sufficient journey of self-healing, shadow work integration, and spiritual growth. To dream shamanically is to dream consciously, astrally aware, and with an intention for healing or wisdom to come through. There are a couple of main themes and features of shamanic dreaming related directly to Pisces.

### Shapeshifting (Power & Spirit Animals)

Pisces is able to shapeshift. Whether it be fairytale-like, magical or other dream characters- or animals resembling spiritual messengers, this watery and empathic sign is able to merge between worlds. This is a trait symbolic of the shaman or people highly shamanically attuned. One is so connected to their astral body, the subtle energy body connected through an etheric cord to the spiritual realms and vastness beyond, that their consciousness floats freely in between worlds; and lifeforms.

Usually this will only happen with specific animals or entities we strongly resonate with. The Shaman's animals are traditionally the OWL, WOLF, and CONDOR. In fact, shamanism has strong roots with many "power animals" and "spirit animals," but these are the ones, from my experience, I found myself interacting with closely once I began to awaken to my shamanic path. This section applies even more strongly with Pisces with strong Scorpio in their charts, such as Moon in Scorpio or Rising Scorpio. Also, Venus in Pisces and/or a Moon in any of the water signs can stimulate such a strong shamanic link.

**The OWL**

Owls symbolize a deep connection and affinity with the astral and ethereal, spiritual and shadow worlds. The owl is wise, intelligent, highly perceptive, and attuned to the subtle realms. Magic flows with the owl, and it is known as a messenger of secrets. The mysteries of the universe can be discovered with the owl's ability to see in the dark, and see beyond the veil of illusion. There's a feminine energy linked to darkness and subconsciousness, the subconscious mind and self. And, with this comes recognition and awareness of the shadow self. Intuition, wisdom of ancestral, ancient and karmic knowledge, and powerful instincts are expanded with and through the owl. OWLS are the shaman's shapeshifting animal of choice because owls can navigate the dreamworlds with ease- effortlessly. This is due to such a strong astral link. Many people and animals don't like the dark, yet owls feel comfortable and at home in darkness. This symbolizes sight, vision and prophecy. One can unveil hidden truths; personal and collective or universal, and hidden secrets, pieces of wisdom and information, and intuitive and instinctive guidance relating to a range of life themes, emotions and energies. Also, seeing through deception and manipulation- your own and others.'

The presence of an owl either as the observer with awareness of being connected to the owl, or actually shapeshifting into an owl, portrays your deep connection to your own shadow self and the intuitive wisdom you draw to help and guide others. Being a Pisces and dreaming of an owl signifies a shamanic cord and link, so this is something to be very mindful of. You may be destined to be a healer, divine and spiritual channel, medium or tarot reader, as explored in the next section ('Embodying 'the Healer''), or you could simply be stepping into new paths of self-leadership and self-empowerment. Clairvoyance, clairsentience, claircognizance and clairaudience are all linked with the owl. The owl also shows that change and transformation are in divine order, such as through a powerful life transition. The general message is that you're being asked to embrace your psychic and intuitive gifts to step into a new journey, a new version of yourself, or some Higher Self connected aspect. One can explore life's mysteries which includes the multiple realms and planes of existence, and quite literally teleport, astral project, and shapeshift at will (if there's a strong and well-developed connection to the owl). It's all about uncovering deeper meanings and truths, increasing self-awareness, and expanding conscious awareness relating to the powers and mystical forces of the energetic-spiritual universe. OWLS brings darkness to light while showing you what it truly means to be a conscious creator and observer of your reality. Unlimited potential too, as feminine energy of darkness and night is strong.

As a Pisces, this has many positive implications. Strengthening your shamanic cord through the healing medicine and wisdom of the owl allows you to access your own soulful gifts and abilities. Qualities & traits that are natural to your sun sign come out and evolve, expand and get a boost, a level-up. The more you work consciously with the owl allowing for the connection, the more you can gain momentum on your true purpose and path. The Owl is essentially one of Pisces' spirit animals anyway, regardless of the shamanic link, as the owl represents the innate connection Pisces has to shadow and subconscious realms. Psychic, clairvoyant, intuitive and imaginative gifts can be increased while the astral body itself can be amplified.

*Key energetic associations*: Intuition, wisdom, instincts, seeing beyond illusions (and deception), uncovering secrets, change and transitions, ancient wisdom and ancestral knowledge, vision and foresight, and prophecy.

**The WOLF**

The wolf is another shamanic animal. This animal represents powerful instincts, feeling, and depth of spirit. There is an intensity with the wolf and it certainly links to the astral and spiritual realms. Mainly, the healing energy is in instinctual responses. This is a powerful spirit animal for Pisces because in their youth and younger years they can often reject their own feelings, sexual needs and desires. Primality and one's "inner animal" is associated with the wolf. Shapeshifting into this animal- or having an ethereal otherworldly dream where you are the observer and you feel an astral or energetic cord the wolf, symbolizes your need to make sense of your emotions and inner instincts. It's important you get in tune with the primal inside you, and further seek to integrate it fully. Sexuality and sensuality are linked to the wolf. The wolf shows us how to embrace our social and family-oriented nature... It's natural to turn towards paths of community and connection, and our instincts are built off of our basic drive for intimacy and connection; emotional and psychological bonding. People with the wolf as their spirit animal tend to be very emotionally intelligent and intuitive. Dependence VS independence is another primary power- life is a balance, and it can be easy to fall into extreme forms of isolation and 'lone wolf' syndrome, especially for Pisces. This is where the term originated: wolves are deeply independent. They symbolize freedom, healthy boundaries, solitude and finding solace in their own power. The wolf has mastered the balance between being a solitary and independent creature connected to their own source of power and intuition, and part of a social community.

Wolves are deeply social creatures too and this is what the balance is referring to. They possess a unique sense of social awareness, wolves can communicate with other members of their pack instinctively and telepathically, after all. They are connected on a subtle and telepathic level. The basic way of saying this is their instincts are super fine-tuned. They have a keen appetite for freedom and being self-sovereign, yet need to feel part of a community or social group simultaneously. This is something Pisces can learn, to overcome any immature (young, from youth) tendencies of extreme solitude and integrate as part of a conscious & loving community. And, to embrace their need for a family one day such as becoming a parent. Many Pisces go so far into the shadow and spiritual realms, or dreamworlds, that they neglect their physical body and reality. Being ruled by Neptune, the planet of dreams, illusions and spirituality, means they often focus so much on psychic and spiritual development, mastering their extrasensory abilities and gifts, that they almost forget about physical things. Family and their place or role in society are two of the things they may neglect. The wolf shows escapist and elusive Pisces the true meaning of belonging to a group, family or community, and losing some of their unwavering independence for balance and harmony. Paying attention to their gut feelings, instincts and deepest desires, whether family or love related, romantic, ambitious or platonic, will let Pisces connect to their true self.

Instincts are the breeding ground for intuition too. When we listen to our emotional and primal needs we open a portal to the Higher Self. This is where the *shamanic essence* of the Wolf comes in; wolves may be highly independent and remind us of the power of community and social connections, but they are first and foremost instinctive creatures with a profound *sixth sense*. They sense things we can't see with our physical eyes, hear sounds and frequencies above and beyond the normal range, and have many subtle and extrasensory gifts.

*Key energetic associations*: Deep and highly evolved instincts, telepathy, sixth sense, intuition, psychic abilities, intelligence, primal urges linking to authenticity, and showing the balance of independence and community/social bonds.


### The CONDOR (+ The EAGLE)

Condors are very similar to Eagles, at least in terms of energetic associations and spiritual symbolism. Many Pisces begin to see Eagles on the astral planes or in dreams when they awaken to their spiritual journey (spiritual gifts included). Both possess the subtle power of sight, vision, and higher self connection. *Intuition*. These birds soar high in the sky and have fine-tuned perception- they are blessed with incredible sight and spiritually this links to vision, foresight, and prophecy. Precognitive abilities are strong in people with the Eagle or Condor as their spirit animal, hence why Pisces often sees or shapeshifts into these birds in dreams. Foresight is the ability to see into the future and they do this advanced and evolved perception, and a deep connection with their instincts and senses.
Multidimensionality is a key message of the Condor and Eagle. Inner sight, DNA activation, spiritual alignment, psychic gifts and self-awareness all come under these birds' healing abilities. And, they can teach the power of creative visualization.

Inspirational qualities increase and expand when these birds start to appear, specifically related to creative, artistic, imaginative and intelligent gifts. They are both intelligent and cerebral and intuitive and spiritual, higher self aligned and attuned.

Destiny, prophecy and understanding too. Everything associated with the higher self and Third Eye and Crown chakras can be learned and integrated. Shapeshifting into any of these symbolizes being connected to your higher self, and cosmic portals of consciousness, subtle dimensions etc. For Pisces, this implies considerable self-discovery and soul integration is in order and available. Sight can be enhanced and understood for imaginative/artistic and spiritual/higher self pathways.

*Key energetic associations*: Intuition, Higher Self, clairvoyance, vision, foresight, imagination, creative inspiration, intelligence, perception, destiny and prophecy.


Beyond shapeshifting and power animals, Shamanic dreaming is similar to lucid dreaming. Pisces draws their power from the cosmos, from the infinite source energy of creation and the universe. Well, this is what shamans do. I myself began to have real (genuine) shamanic experiences, in 2012, before ever reading a book or seeking out Shamanic teachers and masters. My dreams became more magical (ethereal, astrally activated and aware) and multidimensional leading up the 2012 Winter Solstice. This, of course, was the significant timeline shift, the turning of the Ages which is also known as a Grand Cycle Shift. My intuitive, psychic and dream gifts really started to awaken at this time. I also channeled the "blueprint" poem to my debut book just after this celestial transit, in January- March 2013. Like their sister sign Scorpio, Pisces have potential to become natural shamans and energy healers, *if* they should choose to embrace their birth-given powers and step into this role. Not everyone does and this is fine!

## Divine Contact, Superconsciousness; Drawing energy from the Cosmos

One other thing Pisces shares with Shamanism and therefore can be classed under 'Shamanic Dreaming,' is the link to the superconsciousness. Pisces is able to draw energy and healing power from the cosmic, through the astral and spiritual realms. Because Pisces is the 12th sign ruled by Neptune, they are able to act as a channel or conduit for universal and higher consciousness. The body part associated with Pisces is the feet. It is through the feet where one grounds their energy with the planet, with the life force of Mother Earth. Pisces may be spiritual but they are capable of being grounded and responsible, stepping into self-responsibility and a sense of duty (as seen through their opposite sign Virgo), to be of service and let their gifts and unique talents shine. Yet, being ruled by the glyph of the "fish" equally opens them up to cosmic and supernatural energies, including mystical, psychic, subconscious and "higher" energies etc. Thus, Pisces is both of this world and above it. Their feet ground them to the abundant cosmic energy which is channeled through the earth, while their higher self and higher chakras are open to simultaneously receive cosmic energy coming down from above. All in all, Pisces astral body is awakened and active before any healing or self-development work is undertaken. Hence why they're natural lucid and shamanic dreamers, astral projectors, healers and clairvoyants/psychics.

This is largely why many Pisces make wonderful counselors, caregivers, healers or therapists. They draw their wisdom from multiple planes and dimensions of being. They're able to tune into their higher self and the universal insights around, so they can then help others on their journey. Combined with this is the fact Pisces are amazing listeners- they can hold space for others quite naturally. This is the ability to listen and hold space for someone free from judgment. Pisces is non-judgemental, tolerant, patient and understanding to the max, they love people warts and all and see beyond superficial identifications- illusions- to get to the root of a person. Inner beauty and character are more important to Pisces than anything else. Further, they choose to see things from a divine perspective, as opposed to a mundane or ordinary one. Pisces puts the extra in extraordinary, the super in supernatural. They give a dose of magic and mystery rooted in oneness, positivity, and compassion to everything they do, every belief or view they share, and every piece of advice they give. At the highest vibration Pisces is a practical dreamer signifying they can draw from the vast wisdom and awareness of the dreamworlds to inspire, uplift, connect, educate and entertain.

It's easy to assume Pisces is sensitive and overly emotional, yet it's their emotional intelligence and capacity for empathy that provides an opening to connection on a more glamorous, fiery and shining level. Passion defines Pisces. Their charm and magnetism comes from water and the subtle planes, this much is true, however this doesn't take away from their power or charisma. It may be easy to assume Pisces will remain a spaced out, mystical, dreamy and directionless mermaid or merman forever, but inside their skin are vast oceans and galaxies awaiting to be born. At the perfect time. A Pisces may not step into their true path and calling until later in life, from mid to late twenties, early 30s or even later.

Everyone's journey is different and Pisces' path is quite intense if they choose one in harmony with their unique psychic, spiritual or creative gifts. Divine timing and synchronicity features strongly in their life. They're impressionable nature means it can take awhile to find themselves, integrate significant lessons and levels of self-awareness and the like. There is also the growth period as described in the Saturn Return, which is very real and very natural. It's like expecting a baby to run before they can walk, or dismissing the intelligence and genius potential in a fish because it can't climb a tree, like Albert Einstein said. Everything has a cyclic and natural order. Divine timing is a thing. Going back to the fire and glamor, it's important to remember that the sun sign is just one aspect of a person's character & personality. Yes, it is the main one: Sun sign is the core of a person's persona, passions, likes and interests, talents and strengths, yet, there are other significant elements that need considering. Because Pisces is one of the most creative, imaginative and artistically and musically gifted, other aspects in their chart can really make them shine in a fiery, outgoing, or self-expressive way. Fire and air tend to bring out the 'glamor' in the Pisces personality. Allure, excitement, attraction, sparkle, magnetic charisma and mystique... Pisces can embody all of these if they have some strong fire and air placements. They can be very entertaining and more than happy to take the spotlight to share some artistic, musical, or intellectual gift.

The beautiful thing about Pisces is they can know they're extraordinary, a real-life genius, or a self-mastered God or Goddess; and be the most humble person you will ever meet! Pisces has advanced levels of humility and grace. They're compassionate and selfless to the point of idiot compassion (when at their lowest), yet don't feel the need to tell you their achievements or talents, including just how talented or successful they really are. Some people often assume they're talking to someone uninspiring and boring based on just how modest Pisces can be. It's only when one truly gets to know them, or sees them in action, that the Pisces' true potential becomes known. I've personally adopted the viewpoint or self-realization that there are three main paths of a Pisces   and we could shine and thrive in any of these. 1. The caregiver, nurturer and counsellor. 2. The spiritual healer, therapist, psychic and shaman. 3. The multi-talented visionary, creative being, and artistic genius with an advanced imagination. A Pisces at one with themselves with inner harmony and balance is in a perpetual state of universal flow. Giving and receiving. The universe gives to them through gifts and blessings, and Pisces gives back. Pisces shine their light for others and the planet, offering gems of wisdom and inspiration, or healing, kindness and empathy that changes someone's life, and the universe gives back. The spiral is cyclic and repeats itself, thus Pisces' ascended and evolved vibration feeds the universe and the universe returns the favor. Pisces is a very lucky soul. Being the final and 12th sign there's also strong aspects of karma. There's a sense of "coming full circle" associated with Pisces, a return back to Source and spiritual soul alignment. As dreams are a gateway to the soul and psyche, if you're ever in doubt, Pisces, or simply need assistance and guidance; ask your subconscious and the Great Spirit to show you what you need to learn. You have the power of your subconscious mind and the benevolent energies of the universe on your side.

## Embodying 'The Healer'

Finally, many Pisces unconsciously embody the healer, a medicine wo/man who is capable of drawing wisdom, guidance and helpful advice from dream time. Similar to shamanic healing and divine contact Pisces is the sign with healing hands and a healing presence. People sense Pisces' open aura and desire to listen to others. Their empathy and compassion knows no bounds, therefore strangers often come up to this sweet and caring sign to unload their problems, and to open up. Friends and family equally know Pisces is the person to turn to for empathy, understanding and patient non-judgement. Pisces projects an aura or acceptance, kindness and care. They speak subtly, "I am love personified, I will not judge you. I will be your universal reflection and treat you with nothing but empathy and kindness." Or intentions to this effect. Furthermore, just a Pisces' energy alone can be healing. They possess healing presence, a rare type of vibratory frequency that radiates out to create and shape their aura, through their thoughts, emotional intelligence, beliefs, philosophies, and inner impressions. Sometimes they don't need to say anything, as others will change through their being alone. The tone and mood of a room or social gathering will change, and shifts will occur. Pisces' aura (electromagnetic energy field) is POWERFUL- it's strong, large, and influential. You don't need to be an extroverted or gregarious fire sign or a highly chatty and social air sign to create change. Pisces possess an alluring charm and unique personal magnetism, and this arises from their sensitivity, empathy, and yin feminine qualities. Never underestimate the power of the Moon…

As for healing hands, many people born into this sign are natural healers. Divine healing light & energy flows through their hands. They can channel healing energy from the cosmos, ether, and astral planes. Receiving energetic attunements like Reiki or Shamanic attunements and initiations may just be the level up and "extra dose" needed, for they already possess the power and wisdom within. And, expanding on from actually being able to heal others and channel universal life force (healing) energy, they can receive knowledge into people's health and well-being. They can "see"- through psychic and intuitive ability, internal imbalances and ill-health in others, and in plant-life. For example, if a plant is in need of water or to be moved, Pisces will instinctively know. With people and animals they can sense what's going on below the surface. They can feel imbalance, distortion, disharmony and mental, emotional, physical and spiritual ailments without being told anything. Psychic gifts are used for health and divine assistance in many Pisces. In dreams this can manifest as being shown which herbal remedies or plant medicines to advise to a friend (as was the case not long before I stepped into my role as a healer, back in 2014...). My friend's girlfriend at the time suffered from severe menstrual cycle pains. A grandmother character told me which herbal remedy I should recommend to her, and when I did (in waking life) it turns out it was exactly what she needed to hear. Other times I've been shown direct insight into friends' relationships, what emotional blockages and issues they're currently going through, and how their relationships are going.

Not making this about my personal experiences, however, Pisces can see so far and deep beyond the veil that virtually every aspect, element and dimension of someone else's' relationship- or health- is available. One can see when someone is in a beautiful and harmonious relationship, like a true love or soulmate bond, just as they can see when there are jealousies, distortions, and problems regarding trust or possessiveness going on. Toxic and karmic exchanges can be seen as clearly as if it were happening right in front of you. This is Pisces' gift and not so much of a blessing simultaneously; yes, it is amazing to be so divine and "tuned in," but it also leaves us being open to persecution, blame or being labeled as 'crazy' or the like. There's a strong case of "shoot the messenger" with this sign.... I must say, there have been multiple times in life I have seen things, through visions, direct wisdom, and clear dream messages and astral insights, and people have turned against me (for want of better words). It's an integral part of the Pisces journey, therefore, to know when to share their psychic insights and omniscient powers and when to stay silent. It is so tempting to attempt to be everyone's healer, therapist, and free shaman or psychic, but not everyone wants this. It can actually go against the divine flow of things, the natural universal exchange of giving-receiving energy. What does generous, sweet, sincere and self-sacrificing Pisces get in return for invaluable pieces of information and wisdom? Rejection, hatred, and resentment?! It would apparently seem so.

Pisces, be careful of what you share. Dreams can be your golden compass back to your happiness and true north. Be conscious not to disrupt the flow by wanting to give all of you away. Unless your divine insight and powerful knowledge is asked for, requested, or actively sought out- or intuitively offered and responded to with discernment and mindfulness; i.e. you ask a friend if they want to hear what you learned in your dream, or astral projection, and you 'feel the vibe' (clearly, it's a no and your gut can sense this, they wouldn't be that interested and aren't ready for the healing or wisdom)... refrain from sharing. Redirect your new found personal power into your own path. Energize your psychic and clairvoyant self through holding back and keeping the information to yourself, then channeling it into establishing a deeper connection with the dreamspace. This is not selfish as you may like to believe. Remember extreme selflessness and self-sacrifice can be your detriment.

Finally, your whole self identity is tied into the personal and intimate connection in your life, although you will seldom admit this. Isolation and lone wolf syndrome are a message that you're not doing too well. You may be thriving in a few specific areas, but ultimately being cut off for long periods of time is emotionally and psychologically harmful to you. It disconnects you from your source of power and special gifts, a lot of your power and abilities are entwined with how frequently and strongly you can share them. Like the Wolf spirit animal, you need both independence and solitude to make sense of your intuitive senses and intuition, and social bonds and interaction; community, connection, and pathways of family (blood or otherwise, soul family, kindred spirits, etc.) and companionship. Or, at the very least, people to share your divine truth and inspirational insights with. Intuition is like a muscle as well, so it needs to be exercised. Disillusionment and falling into the victim-martyr-rescuer trap can also occur, whilst fantasy may take over reality and depression could become something you get used to. Pisces can learn that mystical and multidimensional, 'otherworldly,' dreams serve a purpose, of course including their insight and healing power, however the lessons should always be brought back to the real world.

## Astrology for the Pisces Soul

Finally, a few key astrological jewels of wisdom I picked up on my journey (which I didn't know back in my youth- and they would have helped me massively), are the significance of Chiron and the South and North Nodes. Chiron is the "Wounded Healer" of astrology, a celestial entity that is not quite a planet but still influences us here on earth (and subconsciously in our dreams). Chiron is a centaur who was wounded deeply. His wounds nearly killed him, however instead of letting them rule his life he transformed them into his "Greatest Teachings." Chiron thus represents our deepest wound and what we can equally do to become the best version of ourselves. A wound is a pathway to healing and wholeness, and to stepping into new positions of leadership and self-empowerment so that we can teach and help others. This is the main message of Chiron: taking your deepest wounds & fears and helping, teaching and inspiring others on their journey. Becoming a wayshower, in other words.

I didn't know, for example, that my Chiron was in Leo. I only discovered this in my early-mid twenties, and this would have helped me significantly from my teens to early twenties. Leo symbolizes creativity and self-expression. Leos are courageous, fiery, passionate, and playful, they're not shy to take the spotlight and step into self-leadership. Leo is also ruled by the 5th house, the house of drama, the Arts, romance, fun and play, creativity, and artistic & imaginative self-expression. So, all of these life themes and traits are affected by a Chiron in Leo. For me, my biggest lesson in life is to embrace my artistic and creative gifts to not shy away from my talents. Basically, to transform fear of being judged and persecuted, rejected and not seen (in terms of creativity) into seizing the day, and further alchemizing my own talents into teaching others or leading by example. Chiron shows us our deepest sensitivities- our vulnerabilities and hidden wounds and fears. I have no regrets on my path, but I certainly would have benefited from knowing this in my youth and early adult life. Your Chiron placement will be unique to you so I highly recommend exploring your Natal (Birth) chart.

*The Centaur (Chiron) is secretly struggling with deep pain- an unseen wound, but he's transformed this pain to help others. Thus, he draws his inner strength from his wound in order to be a way shower and teacher, or helper and healer.*

The North and South Nodes are extremely beneficial to be aware of too. These are also known as Lunar Nodes and they are the key to finding your true path and what you need to leave behind. This is really useful to know as a Pisces, and can provide for some great self-discovery and conscious exploration in the dreamworlds. The North and South Nodes. They relate to the Moon and are directly opposite each other, together forming the 'Nodal Axis.' The north and south nodes aren't planetary bodies, but specific points defined by angles that take into account the relationship between the Sun, Moon and Earth at our time of birth, therefore in our natal chart. Lunar nodes are the points where the Moon's orbit interests the plane of the 'ecliptic,' essentially. Ultimately they symbolize karma, our personal karmic balance. The North Node represents the experiences we attract and are most likely to attract in this lifetime. It helps us grow spiritually, emotionally, psychologically and physically, also providing a foundation for lessons and opportunities for growth rooted in the material world. It can be seen as one's destiny, legacy and sense of service. The placement of the North Node determines what you may be destined to do and achieve in this lifetime, what type of skills and gifts you will possess and develop, and how, if and when you ground these talents into a vocation, calling or profession. Knowing your North Node adds an extra dimension of self-awareness and self-knowledge to your Pisces nature.

The South Node refers to our sense of belonging and comfort, what we are used to and "fall back on." The South Node is our natural strength, talents, abilities and somewhat over-developed traits. They are the behaviors, gifts and patterns we are used to. Gifts & abilities associated with the South Node come naturally to us, yet it can result in an imbalanced and extreme type of personality. MY South Node, for example, is in Cancer- the sign of family, roots and emotional sensitivity. My lesson in life is to transcend emotional attachments and past cycles, patterns of behavior and mindsets that don't serve my growth or highest potential. Basically, let go of my emotional safetynet and comfort blanket! Cancer is the nurturer and caregiver who is reliant on family and intimate bonds, but with this comes codependency (at a lower vibration). The message of the South Node is to transcend and evolve past the familiarity and comforts; we're supposed to steer more towards the North Node, seeking to embody the qualities and opportunities of the lunar North Node symbolism and energy, while becoming less dependent on the South Node's energy. Attachment is something we need to release if we wish to step into our true power, path and mature adult body. This may be attachment to people, places, experience, possessions, beliefs, ideas or philosophies, the key is that we commit to self-evolution. *Transcendence.*

The South Node can be seen as a childhood toy that has become dirty and torn, yet we desperately hold onto it- even though we know it has out-served its purpose. Letting go is key. The north node would be a masterpiece of a musical creation, book, or movie book which you've been creating and putting together for years. This song, book or movie reflects your legacy and the encompassing gems of wisdom, reflections and life learnings, for you to share with others.... Which do you hold onto, Pisces, the dirty torn toy or the masterpiece of a creation? Future generations can be inspired and heal from your North Node actions and self-acceptance, yet clinging onto the past doesn't serve anyone. Ultimately, the North Node relates to achievements, successes, accomplishment and self-mastery of gifts and talents. So not reaching your full potential implies your true self may be imbalanced and neglected, in need of integration. It's important to take steps towards healing and embodying the characteristics of one's North Node so they can live up to their full destiny. The North Node is where you're going and heading to, your Higher Self, Future Self, and Adult Self. The South Node is where you've been- childhood, youth, and your past. As the Old Soul and 12th & final sign, this is important to you more than anyone, dear One.

# About the Author

**Grace Gabriella Puskas** is a spiritual author of two groundbreaking collections of poetry and a creative visionary. She is a qualified Reiki Master Teacher, Dream therapist, Crystal & Shamanic Healer, Chi Kung practitioner, Reflexologist, Aromatherapist, and Herbalist. In 2014 she won the Local Legend Spiritual Writing Competition, resulting in the publication of her debut book of poetry, 'A Message from Source.' Throughout her twenties she spent her time volunteering on various projects, spiritual, conscious, eco/sustainable, community, and animal welfare and conservation; she has lived on organic farms, shamanic land communities, and in ashrams, and has created beautiful Medicinal herb gardens, in addition to leading workshops in the Healing Arts & Spirituality. Grace Gabriella works at festivals and conscious community gatherings where she offers therapies, healing, and workshops aimed at spiritual development and accessing creative, soul, and intuitive/psychic gifts. She is a Teacher of the Healing Arts, Reiki, and Creative & Spiritual Development, and a poet, wordsmith, world-class ghost-writer, philosopher, inspired visionary, soul guide, psychic, empathic counselor, and astrologer. She is also a Pisces with a grand water trine and grand earth trine in her birth chart (two rare astrological alignments). Grace believes we can transcend comfort zones by leaving behind a fear timeline, and moving towards a timeline of LOVE. Unity consciousness, authentic and conscious spirituality, holistic health, and healing planetary consciousness as well as Mother Earth, beautiful Gaia, are her main life goals and service. She is a Medicine Woman and free-flow Musician who embodies elements of a modern-day, grounded, mystic.

✧

**gracegabriella33@gmail.com**

I also have lots of FREE wisdom-audios and consciousness-expanding poetry on my Youtube channel, *The Dream & Spirit Weaver*.

gracegabriella33.wixsite.com/grace
www.youtube.com/@TheDreamSpiritWeaver

✧

# PISCES POETRY

You can find my "blueprint" poem to and for the Piscean Spirit on Youtube,
PISCES POETRY- Learn Astrological Compatibility, Learn Astrology! ✧
**#PiscesPoetry #OldSouls**

*Link here[1]*

---

[1] https://www.youtube.com/watch?v=blfSpnOkSDI&t=88s

# Afterword

If you've enjoyed this book, please check out my other books!

<u>A Message from Source</u>: 33 poems exploring consciousness, our connection to one another, and the universe as a whole. *My debut book won the Local Legend National Writing Competition in 2014.*

<u>A Story of One</u>: A sequel to *A Message from Source*, which delves into tantra, mysticism, healing, higher consciousness, love, intimacy, friendship, community, and soulmate bonds.

<u>Spirit Animals of the Star Signs: Power Animals of the Zodiac</u>: With 52 reviews at the time of writing this book, this game changing "one-of-a-kind" book on spirit animals and astrology was written during my travels through South America in 2022. I began writing in the sacred Mayan lands of Mexico, continued in the mountainous rainforests of Monteverde Costa Rica, and finished in the Amazon Jungle in Ecuador. This book is so in depth it's been described as the holy grail of guides!

<u>Mental Health Issues of the Star Signs & Zodiac: Let's Get Triggered, Heal, and Evolve... Together</u>: Another 2023 release, this is one of my MOST triggering books, as it's a deep sea dive into the places not many of us want to explore. Hint: My Higher Self triggered me during the creation process. That's how intense it is… *Not for the faint-hearted.*

<u>52 Tantric Tips for Ultimate Intimacy from an Energy Master: Exploring Tantric Intimacy; Merging the Lower Primal Self and Higher Spiritual Self for Your Best Sex Life!</u>- As the title signifies…

<u>EMPATH Essential Survival Guide!</u>- A Complete Guide to The Empath Blueprint, Overcoming Narcissistic Abuse, Reclaiming Self-Sovereignty, and Color & Chakra Therapy and Healing.

*If you have the paperback copy, all of these books can be found on Amazon! <3*

# A GRAND WATER TRINE

A grand water trine symbolizes a highly idealistic, insightful, and dreamy personality. Balanced and harmonic resonance occurs, and the individual has a strong pull towards peace. There's a peace-loving, just, and harmonious disposition, and someone with a grand water trine will be very psychic and intuitive. They are gifted in the realms of art, music, the imagination, and all forms of creativity & self-expression. They're also deeply empathic, compassionate, nurturing and kind, with many spiritual gifts. Soul is present. This person isn't short of talent either! Multi-talentedness runs deep, whilst the triple water element makes them incredibly adaptable, chameleon-like. They will be empathic and clairvoyant to the point of telepathy and other advanced forms of communication. Connection is their primary goal in life, and they will seek to inspire others through their creative, caring, and spiritual gifts.

A grant water trine signifies spiritual awakening and a path towards enlightenment. Divinity and religious and/or spiritual themes feature strongly in their life. They believe in the power of human connection, of Spirit, and of service to a greater or higher cause. Purpose fills their life. Intimacy is craved, but it is rooted in a recognition of the mental, emotional, physical and spiritual bodies & planes; a holistic and encompassing approach is taken to life and self. Astral connection and visions are possible, also a regular occurrence in this person's life. They may be gifted clair-sentiently, clair-audiently, and clairvoyantly, and dreams are a direct link to the subconscious and divine inspiration. Wisdom and healing too.

Cancer represents amazing gifts of nurturance, empathy, care and a sense of belonging. This water sign brings the energy of powerful instincts that can create harmony and unity. Scorpio symbolizes intensity and depth, an alignment with Soul and spiritual & intuitive gifts. Also, diving deep into the shadow realms (and the light and wisdom that arises there). Pisces is the Old Soul embodying traits & qualities from all 12 star signs. Pisces awakens compassion and unconditional love while providing portrayals to higher conscious and advanced creative, musical and imaginative gifts. A Grand Water Trine occurs when the 3 water signs are in 120° angles to one another. It visually looks like a diamond when pictured holistically with the other aspects of the chart.

Finally, emotions define and rule this person's life. Their primary desires are rooted in a need for emotional connection and bonding on a deep level. Honesty, loyalty, sincerity, a vivid inner life, tolerance, understanding, artistry, and unlimited creative potential are other key characteristics.

**Key information about the author:**

Grace was born on 14th March 1992 at 8:22am, in Sunset Boulevard, Los Angeles, California. She shares the same birth date as Albert Einstein, has a Grand Water Trine *and* Grand Earth Trine in her natal chart, and is a Life Path 11. Life Path 11 is the Master Intuitive and Illuminator; she is also an Expression/Destiny Number 22, another master number, with her Moon in Cancer, Rising/Ascendant in Taurus, and Venus in Pisces. Her Soul Urge/Heart's Desire is numerology 3. For any real astrology fanatics, she has her Mars in Aquarius, Mercury in Aries, and North Node in Capricorn. Her Chiron is in Leo.

Printed in Great Britain
by Amazon

39580493R00064